The Good Dog Library

Train Your Dog Right

Basic Obedience, Skill Building & Problem Solving

ISBN: 1-9758716-1-7

Tufts Media Enterprises, LLC
169 Holland St.
Somerville, MA 02144 USA

Train Your Dog Right: Basic Obedience,
Skill Building & Problem Solving
The editors of Your Dog

ISBN: 1-9758716-1-7
1. Dogs-Training   2. Canine   3. Canine Training

Manufactured in the United States of America

The Good Dog Library

Train Your Dog Right

Basic Obedience, Skill Building & Problem Solving

Scientific Editor: Alice Moon-Fanelli

Clinical Assistant Professor
Tufts University School of Veterinary Medicine
North Grafton, MA

Contents

Section III: Training Tools

Introduction

Choosing a canine companion is not unlike choosing a mate. Of course there must be a physical attraction, but even more importantly, you must share common interests, temperaments, and energy levels. The two best ways to prevent a breakdown in later relations between people and their canine companions are 1) thoughtful selection of a canine companion who suits an owner's personality and lifestyle and 2) appropriate early training and socialization.

Most dogs are not "born" with behavior problems; they just find themselves in an environment that is inadequate for their needs and in the company of owners who do not prepare and work with their canines to adapt the dog's behavior to their needs and expectations.

If loyalty, a cooperative work ethic, and affectionate nature appeal to you, a quality Golden Retriever might be well suited for you. If you admire independence, creativity, and high energy, you might find a Basenji to be irresistibly fascinating. Carefully researching a breed's behavioral predisposition is more important than selecting a dog based on physical attractiveness, popularity or presumed convenience. While you might gravitate toward the appearance and intelligence of a Border Collie, if you live in an urban environment or work long hours, your "unemployed" Border Collie most likely won't provide you with the type of companionship you were longing for.

The amount and quality of time you invest during the first year of your dog's life is extremely important to ensure that he or she is behaviorally equipped to adapt to both your lifestyle and your future expectations. If you aspire to start a family, make sure your puppy associates children of all ages with positive experiences. If you travel frequently, locate a quality daycare-boarding facility and acclimate your dog to this environment early on. Finally, all dogs need to be taught manners to become canine good citizens.

While we all are entertained by and tend to indulge puppy antics, envision how these behaviors will play out when the dog is mature. While the mouthing and jumping up that your ten-week-old Great Dane engages in might amuse you now, how pleasurable will this behavior be when he is full grown? Laying the proper groundwork in that crucial first year, labor intensive as it may seem to be, will allow you to relax the rules later in your dog's life.

In today's society, our canine companions have taken on a new role in our lives and are often revered as family members. With this new role has come a tendency for indulgence and unrealistic expectations based on excessive anthropomorphism. Dogs will be dogs, and therein lies the misunderstanding and miscommunication that results in strained relations between owners and their animals. Understanding species-typical canine behavior and the tendency for individual breeds to display distinct and sometimes accentuated aspects of canine behavior is essential to forming a mutually respectful human-animal bond.

Dogs are not children, and not all dogs offer unconditional love. Desire for unconditional love promotes overfeeding (food is love) and inhibits owners from laying ground rules for mannerly behavior. Mutual respect and communication developed through proper training and education are essential to forming a solid relationship with any companion animal.

Consider the characteristics you find most admirable in a boss. Do you work better for an employer who is constantly critical and upping the ante without due reward? Or are you more likely to give your all to a leader who compliments your honest efforts and benevolently guides you in a manner that allows you to improve the quality of your work? For most of us, the answer is obvious and so it goes with our canine companions as well. Be fair. Be honest. Be a leader you would want to follow.

This book focuses on positive training methods to ensure that you and your dog enjoy a quality life together. You'll find clear, understandable advice on training challenges nearly every owner faces—rechanneling excessive barking; working on the basic yet essential commands; and proper etiquette with unfamiliar people and dogs. If your dog's already a pro at the basics, you'll find information on events and competitions such as flyball and agility testing.

Whether you want your dog to excel in training or simply behave in a civilized manner, the positive training methods espoused in this book bring out the best in all of us. Remember, learning stops when punishment begins, and aggression tends to beget aggression. Be a teacher, not a tyrant. ■

Alice Moon-Fanelli
Clinical Assistant Professor
Tufts University School of Veterinary Medicine
July 2004

Section I

Basic Training

1

Choosing the Right Training Medium

Print? Video? Cyberspace? Live and in person?
Solo or group? Your choices are legion.

Today there are more dog-training options than ever before. In addition to group and private classes, you can choose from hundreds of books, reams of magazine articles, dozens of videos, and numerous dog-training sites on the Web. But which medium best suits you and your dog?

Clarifying your objectives can help you decide which instructional tool to select. If you've never trained a dog before and want to teach your dog to obey the indispensable "Sit," "Stay," and "Come" commands, a basic obedience class might be most useful.

If you're training your dog for competition—in obedience or one of the many canine working or athletic events—you'll probably benefit from the extra help that subject-specific books and videos provide.

If you are seeking to solve minor canine foibles such as pulling on lead or jumping, any instructional tool—properly selected and applied—can help. However, solving more serious behavior problems such as separation anxiety or aggression may require one-on-one sessions with a qualified trainer or animal behaviorist.

Another important criterion for selecting a training tool is the trainer's philosophy. No matter which training tool you choose, make sure the techniques emphasize positive reinforcement—such as praise and play—rather than punishment. "That way, you'll have a dog that wants to work for you rather than a dog that's afraid of you," notes Dr. Linda Aronson, a veterinary behavioral consultant in Norfolk, Massachusetts. If you disagree with the trainer's approach, don't buy the book or video or sign up for the class. Avoid trainers or training materials that promise quick fixes.

Print, Tape, CD, DVD, or Cyberspace?

As you're mulling over training-media options, keep in mind that every vehicle has both pluses and minuses. Tapes, CDs,and DVDs show you techniques in action, and you can replay them repeatedly to review specific material.

Visual media also are useful if you and your dog need to brush up on previously learned skills. But before investing in a training tape, CD, or DVD, consider whether the medium fits your personal learning style. If you've learned successfully from cooking or skiing tape, try a dog-training via a visual means. But if your instructional tapes, CDs, and DVDs collect dust, consider a book or a class.

With books, it's easy to know what you're getting before you buy. Unlike videos, where you're usually at the mercy of promotional blurbs on the covers, books give you the freedom to thumb through and see what's inside. Also, most books contain more information than will fit into a single video script. Books are also more portable than videos.

As for the Internet, a word of caution: anyone can post information on the Web, so check out the trainer's qualifications and credentials before using any methods you find in cyberspace.

Live and In Person: Your Best Bet

Although books and videos can be helpful dog-training adjuncts, there's nothing like a class with a competent trainer. A trainer can watch you work with your dog, tailor techniques to fit both of you, and answer your questions.

Classes also provide an opportunity for socialization with other dogs, a vital element in canine behavioral development. The presence of other dogs and people also provides real-life distractions that help test the skills your dog is learning.

Plus, knowing that you both have to "perform" each week in front of a group may motivate you to work more diligently with your dog on your own—a key to training success.

But dog training classes vary widely in style and quality of instruction. It is important to do research and make an informed choice before selecting a trainer. Before putting your dog's future in a trainer's hands, we recommend that you ask a lot of questions. Look for a trainer who has had experience handling hundreds or thousands of dogs and who has taught classes for at least two years. There are very few reputable dog trainer certification programs. While ongoing education is vital for a professional trainer, a brief certification course cannot provide a would-be trainer with the necessary experience brought by years of dog handling and training.

Find out where the trainer trained. His or her experience should total at least several years of exposure to a variety of breeds. Find out what other activities are available, if not through this specific trainer, then through other trainers and dog clubs in the area. Ask if the training methods used will prepare you for the other activities that capture your interest.

When you find the style that appeals to you, watch a class before you enroll. Dogs and owners should appear to be enjoying themselves; if they aren't, you probably won't either.

Make sure you like the methods the trainer uses. If you see something that makes you uncomfortable, a harsh punishment, for example, ask the trainer after the class whether what you witnessed is par for the course. The trainer might regard the method as "necessary" for most dogs—or a rare occurrence prompted by the failure of other methods. Trust your instincts about the response you receive.

Investigating Instructors

Since there are no universal certification standards, academic degree requirements, or licensing regulations, anyone can call himself or herself a dog trainer. How do you select a reputable instructor?

■ *Seek references from dog-owning friends, your veterinarian, or your local humane society.*

■ *Personally investigate a trainer's techniques by auditing a class without your dog.*

■ *Watch all participants. If you see angry, frustrated people and cowering canines, look elsewhere.*

■ *Look for a trainer who gives individualized attention and tailors methods to fit different dogs and people.*

You Get What You Pay For

Be cautious of classes offered by dog clubs and large chain pet stores. They are often less expensive than those taught at privately owned dog training schools, but they also frequently are taught by members who may or may not have any previous teaching experience. These classes are often large with little individualized attention. Many club classes use force-based training only. Chain pet stores may advertise positive reinforcement, but often hire novices with little or no training knowledge or experience. They also tend to have high turnover, since quality trainers can do better on their own.

The cost of dog training can vary widely. Free courses sometimes can be found through clubs or city recreation departments. Just remember, you get what you pay for. Group classes that meet once a week can range from as little as $45 to $125 or more for a six- to eight-week course. The price generally reflects cost of living in the area. Expect an average of six to eight people and their dogs in the class; larger classes should have assistants to help the trainer offer each of the students at least a little individualized attention. This type of multiweek course is almost always paid for in advance.

Many trainers also offer private instruction at their school or, sometimes, at your home. Expect to pay from $45 to $150 an hour for this type of one-on-one session. During a one-hour consultation for a specific behavior challenge, your trainer should demonstrate one or more approaches for resolving the behavior and watch you apply the tech-

Knowing that you both have to "perform" each week in front of a group may motivate you to work more diligently with your dog on your own—a key to training success.

niques. You can also expect the trainer to offer options for an ongoing program for you and your dog.

Going to Class

Once you select a trainer but before you attend the first class, try to have a brief discussion with the person in charge. Make sure he or she is aware of your goal for the class to prevent any misunderstandings regarding the intensity (or lack thereof!) with which you pursue perfection in your dog.

First, you must decide what you want from a training class. Class styles vary, with the two primary approaches being the military-style precision training traditionally used for showing in the obedience ring, and family dog classes that are more concerned with teaching canine good manners and social skills.

The easiest way to tell the difference between the two is to ask what equipment is required. If the answer is "a choke chain, slip collar, training collar, or prong collar," the class is probably the more formal obedience class that relies on the use of force and physical correction. If the answer is "a flat buckle collar or a head collar," you have found the more relaxed family dog class that uses positive reinforcement, rewards (treats) and praise rather than jerks on a collar to train the dog.

Remember, practicing at home needn't be drudgery. "Once you know the basic techniques, you can use everyday interactions—such as feeding, grooming, and playing—as opportunities to reinforce training," Dr. Aronson says.

Don't hesitate to excuse yourself and walk out of a class if you are told to do something to your dog that makes you feel uncomfortable. It can be difficult and embarrassing to disagree with a trainer, especially in front of an entire class, but remember, it's your relationship with your dog and the trust the two of you share that are important, not someone else's opinion. There will always be another class and another day to get it right.

Trainers and classes vary in focus, intensity, and cost. Be sure to find an environment that you and your dog enjoy. ∎

2

Different Strokes

*Training techniques are many and varied.
We can help you choose the right
approach for your dog.*

One sunny summer day, you're taking a stroll around the neighborhood. You pass a park and notice a dog training class in progress. The instructor is standing in a meadow with a number of dogs and owners positioned in a large circle. Each dog is wearing a shiny chain collar. From time to time when a dog lunges ahead or lags behind, the owner jerks on the leash to bring the dog back to heel position, then pets and praises the animal. You hear an occasional "No!" issued in a commanding tone. The dogs appear well-behaved, and all of them are doing the same thing at precisely the same time.

You continue on, and reach another park where you see another training class. This is a more ragged-looking bunch, although also well-behaved. A half-dozen dogs are walking in different directions with their owners, turning, stopping and starting up again apparently at random. The dogs are wearing regular flat collars. Some of them also wear something around their noses that looks like a muzzle, but on closer inspection you realize it is more like a horse halter. There is no jerking, but there is much treat-tossing and talking; you hear a lot of "Yes!" and an occasional odd clicking noise. Since you have been thinking about signing your dog up for training, you pause to ponder the differences between the two groups.

Both groups are beginning dog training classes. Both can produce well-trained dogs. The main differences are the training methods and the philosophies and behavior theories behind those methods.

The Training Continuum

All dog training techniques fit somewhere on a continuum with seriously harsh and abusive punishment-based methods at one extreme to pure positive reinforcement at the other. Neither extreme is likely to be very practical or effective, nor will you find many trainers who recommend using only methods from one extreme or the other. Most trainers use a combination of techniques that place them somewhere between the two extremes, depending on whether they are primarily compulsion-based or primarily positive-based.

Within the dog-training community the debate about methods is generally good-natured, albeit spirited. Hackles get raised when trainers become strident about on the very best method to resolve a particular canine behavior challenge.

Why the diversity? Because numerous approaches can successfully teach a dog to do what we ask and because people bring an infinite number of philosophical, cultural, emotional, and ideological differences to the dog-training profession.

The number of styles available can make things a little confusing when you look for a trainer or an obedience class. Would you know what an instructor meant if he or she said the program was all about "positive punishment and compulsion training?" Or if another trainer told you that he or she teaches only "clicker training?"

What follows will provide you with definitions for these terms, and more. You'll be able to talk training with people from all schools of canine behavior modification and find the class format that works best for your and your dog.

Behavioral Theories

In behavioral terms, training is known as "conditioning behavior." We don't teach new behaviors with training; after all, our dogs already know how to sit, lie down, stay in one place, walk by our side, or come running to us from far away—when they want to. It's just that they may not know how to do it (or may not choose to do it) when we ask them to. Training is conditioning (or teaching) a dog to reliably give us the behaviors we ask for, when we ask for them.

Classical conditioning

As first described by Pavlov, there is an association between a stimulus and a response, or behavior. (A stimulus is something that elicits a response.) This is the famous "ring a bell, the dog salivates," experiment that most of us learned about in high school psychology classes. Classical conditioning can generally be used to teach only very simple behaviors.

Operant conditioning

This method is most commonly used for training because it can be used to teach complex behaviors and behavior "chains," a series of behaviors strung together. With operant conditioning, there is an association between a behavior and its consequence. The dog does something, then something happens as a result of the behavior. There are four ways that this works. Two are labeled positive, which means, in this usage, that the dog's behavior makes something appear. Two are labeled negative, which means the dog's behavior makes something go away. The "something" may be pleasant or unpleasant.

■ Positive reinforcement: The dog's behavior makes something good happen. For example, when the dog walks next to you without pulling on the leash, he or she gets a treat (treat = good thing).

■ Positive punishment: The dog's behavior makes something bad happen. If the dog pulls on the leash, his or her neck gets jerked to bring the animal back to heel position (jerk on neck = bad thing).

■ Negative punishment: The dog's behavior makes something good go away. When the treat is used as a lure to keep the dog walking in heel position, he or she may jump up to get it. The treat is hidden until the jumping stops. Once the dog stays on the ground, the treat is offered. (treat = good thing; hidden = "goes away").

■ Negative reinforcement: The dog's behavior makes something bad go away. A no-pull harness puts pressure on the dog's chest as long as the dog puts pressure on the leash. When the dog stops pulling, the pressure stops. (pressure = bad thing; no pulling = bad thing "goes away").

Compulsion Training

Traditional compulsion-based training works on the philosophy that we have to show the dog who is boss. The animal must do what we say, and quickly. Otherwise, correction follows immediately, or the dog will learn that he or she can ignore our commands. The primary tool for compulsion trainers is positive punishment (the dog's behavior makes something bad happen, like a jerk on the leash), often followed by a treat, a pat, and/or verbal praise to keep up the dog's enthusiasm for the training process. Twenty years ago, the use of food treats as praise was abhorrent to traditional trainers.

Compulsion training works, as demonstrated by decades of well-behaved dogs. Proponents argue that the small amount of discomfort that the dogs experience is worth the end result of a reliable, promptly responsive dog, and skilled trainers use the minimum amount of force necessary to get the job done. But this approach can be problematic with very dominant or independent dogs who don't take kindly to being pushed and pulled around and who may decide to argue back. People who take this approach must be prepared to use enough force to get their message across quickly, and be willing to escalate the level of force if necessary.

Advocates of compulsion-based training argue that the small amount of discomfort that a dog experiences is worth the result—a reliable, promptly responsive dog.

Potentially dangerous techniques like "scruff shakes" and "alpha rolls" work only if the trainer is strong enough to persevere if the dog fights back. Keep in mind learning stops once such punishment begins. Even if the owner is willing and able, this still is not a productive tactic. Many owners and trainers are either unwilling or unable to use this kind of force with their dogs.

Timid, submissive or sensitive dogs may also not do well with positive punishment. Forceful corrections can cause them to "melt down," and miscalculations can cause damage to the owner's or trainer's relationship with the dog.

Yet another concern about compulsion training is the possible damage to a dog's throat from a standard choke chain collar, which can exert tremendous pressure on the trachea. These collars are not recommended for puppies under the age of six months, yet it is more and more widely accepted that starting puppies in training classes at the age of 10 weeks is ideal, to take advantage of a pup's critical socialization and learning period.

Clicker Training

"Clicker trainers" is a slang term for individuals who use positive reinforcement as their method of choice, combined with an **audible signal** to indicate the desired behavior. These trainers prefer to induce dogs to offer the desired behavior voluntarily, then mark and reward the animals when they do so. The **marker signal**, or "bridge," can be the Click! of the clicker, a whistle, some other mechanical sound, or a word. "Yes!" is frequently used to mark a correct behavior. Behaviors that are ignored (not rewarded) tend to go away, or "extinguish." Since all living creatures tend to repeat behaviors that are rewarding, behaviors that are repeatedly marked and rewarded by a dog's owner get offered more and more frequently.

Take, for example, the puppy who wants to jump up on everyone. Dogs greet each other face to face, so it is natural for our dogs to want to greet our faces. When they are cute little puppies, we pick them up and cuddle them in our arms, rewarding them for being "up." Small wonder that so many dogs jump on people!

Many of the suggested compulsion approaches to correcting jumping behavior actually reward the very behavior we are trying to extinguish. When the dog jumps up, he or she touches us. That's a reward. We make eye contact, another reward. We pay attention to the animal by telling him or her to get off. That's a reward. We reach

down to push the dog away. Touch—another reward! For some
rowdy dogs, even a knee in the chest is an invitation to start a rous-
ing game of body slam.

The positive reinforcement approach (the dog's behavior makes
something good happen) relies on the principle that ignored behaviors will extinguish. But how do you ignore an enthusiastic
canine who is leaping up to greet you nose to nose, inflicting multiple bruises and lacerations in the process? Just standing still
doesn't work; he or she gets all kinds of rewards by jumping all
over you.

Instead, we turn our back on the dog and step away. As the dog
tries to come around to face us, we do it again. Turn away and step
away, over and over. Sooner or later (and with most dogs this happens much sooner than you would imagine) the dog gets frustrated
and confused, and sits down to puzzle out your bizarre behavior.
Bingo! Now you turn toward the dog, say "Yes!" and offer a treat
from the stash that you keep in your pockets in anticipation of opportunities just like this. You can also pet and praise your dog. If he
she jumps up again, repeat the process. The theory goes that before

*Years ago using
a treat as a
reward or incen-
tive was frowned
upon by many
trainers. Today,
the method is
widely accepted.*

you know it, the dog will understand that to get the desired attention quickly as possible, it works best to sit, not jump, when you approach.

The latter approach also uses negative punishment: the dog's behavior (jumping up) causes something good (you) to go away. Then, when the dog sits and you offer a treat and attention, it is positive reinforcement—the dog's behavior (sitting) causes something good (treat and attention) to happen.

Clicker trainers use primarily positive reinforcement, but will also use varying degrees of negative punishment, negative reinforcement, and positive punishment, depending on the dog and the individual trainer's own comfort and skill levels.

Proponents of positive reinforcement training say that a training approach based on rewards rather than punishment builds trust in the human-canine relationship and encourages the dog to think for himself or herself and make deliberate choices of rewardable behavior rather than living in fear of punishment. Proponents of the approach state that dogs trained with these methods tend to be more willing to think for themselves, choose "right" behaviors, take risks, and offer new behaviors than do dogs who have been physically corrected for making mistakes.

Prevention

Of course, it is not always possible to ignore a dog's inappropriate behavior. Some unwanted behaviors are self-rewarding, destructive or unsafe, such as barking at the mail carrier, chewing electrical cords or chasing cars. Management should be the first solution. It is easier to prevent unwanted behaviors than it is to correct them. It is far easier to keep your dog properly confined in a fenced yard or on a leash than it is to stop a dog with a strong prey drive from chasing cars, cats, joggers or skateboarders. While you manage the behavior, you also work to train a better level of control so the dog becomes more reliable around highly enticing stimuli.

NRM

Another approach is the use of a "No Reward Marker" or NRM. The NRM is a signal to let the dog know she made a mistake. It is not applied angrily, just used in a neutral tone to let the dog know that the behavior didn't earn a reward.

Commonly used NRMs include "Oops," "Try again," or the sound "Uh!" or "At!" A properly used NRM tells the dog that the behavior offered was not the behavior requested, and encourages the dog to try again.

Yet another positive behavior-correction method is to ask for (and reward) an incompatible behavior. A dog can't lie on a favorite rug in the living room and bark at the visitor on the front porch at the same time. If we teach the dog that the doorbell is the cue to go lie down on the rug and stay there, your guest will no longer be greeted with the dog's sometimes unwelcome exuberance.

Positive Reinforcement

Anyone can use the basic principles used by scent dog trainers to obtain quicker, happier compliance from their own dogs. Keep these basic principles in mind:

■ *Love and respect are crucial. Your dog needs to know that you're on the same side. "I had a dog in my last group that just would not open up to me," says former U.S. Department of Agriculture trainer Sandy Seward. "I spent probably the first week sitting in his kennel run with him. I had a Nylabone and he had a Nylabone, and we played Nylabone games. Once I got this dog to respect me and to relate to me, I found him to be more pliable in training."*

■ *Varying your rewards helps motivate your dog. A dog who doesn't know which fantastic reward to expect will keep working his or her hardest. Give extra-special rewards ("jackpots") when the dog does something particularly outstanding, but occasionally throw in a jackpot for an average response. Other times, withhold rewards until you get an excellent performance. That way you the dog is stimulated to work harder to get a greater reward.*

■ *Being afraid to move backward can often impede a trainer. Deciding to move forward with a lesson too quickly can stop a dog's progress. "A lot of times that's interpreted as the dog's inability to comprehend, but it's usually the trainer who has moved too quickly," Seward says. Step back and review previous lessons to make sure your dog fully understands and is comfortable with what you're asking.*

The Ongoing Debate

There is no lack of debate between trainers about the effectiveness of the various training approaches. Take the case of an aggressive dog. Compulsion trainers believe that such a dog must be physically corrected for the least sign of aggression: hackles raised, intense stare, growling. This teaches the dog that the behavior is not acceptable.

Positive reinforcement trainers suggest that a better approach is to change the way the dog thinks about the aggression-causing stimulus by associating it with positive things. If the dog's instinct is to get aggressive around children, for instance, the trainer might quickly give the dog a treat every time children are encountered, so the dog will begin to associate the presence of children with "Good things happen," and the aggression will fade. Aggressive behavior is not lurking beneath the surface, because the dog no longer thinks of children as threats; they are now a source of good things.

Clicker trainers tend to believe that force-based training dampens a dog's enthusiasm for learning. Compulsion trainers often express the view that reward-trained dogs won't perform reliably under stress. Clicker trainers say that violence begets violence, and that many dogs who are euthanized for biting were made worse by physical corrections. Compulsion trainers argue that their methods are faster, and that sometimes the use of force can cause quicker behavior changes that save a dog's life whose owner is at the breaking point and on the verge of sending the dog to the shelter.

Deciding on what training methods to use is up to the owners, but they can look to their dogs for help in making the choice. We can find pet dogs and obedience show ring competitors from both training styles who are happy, reliable, willing workers, and we can find dogs from both training styles who are poorly trained and out of control.

However, there seem to be better results with the non-force-based methods. Much larger percentages of dogs in compulsion-based classes grudgingly comply with commands or look bored or disgruntled than in positive reinforcement classes, where enthusiasm usually abounds among all students in the class, two-legged and four-legged. Many pet owners, left to their own devices, are more likely to follow their hearts and choose a gentle, non-violent training methods, while those owners conditioned by past trainers and the pressure of competition who believe that a little "pop on the collar" won't hurt the dog, will more quickly accept force-based training.

Now let's go back to our imaginary stroll around the neighborhood. You're ready to sign up for a class, and just have to decide which one. Just put yourself in your dog's place for a moment and ask yourself which kind of class he or she would prefer. There's your answer. ■

3

The Best Start

Starting off on the right foot is critical!
Here's a primer on what you can accomplish during
those important first few weeks.

They look so cute, so needy. Maybe you've just acquired a perfect pudge of a yellow Labrador retriever puppy—eight weeks old, fat, round and chunky with a shiny black button nose, warm brown eyes and milk-sweet puppy breath. Or maybe you've been charmed by an older dog you met through a shelter, rescue organization, a friend, or a family member.

No matter how lovable your "new" dog is, those first few weeks in your home will be critical. Older dogs may need training to help with bad habits they picked up earlier in life. Puppies eight weeks and older can benefit from learning the do's and don'ts of your house.

Coming Home

A common mistake of novice dog owners is to give the new arrival too much freedom. The first few weeks of puppyhood in particular are a critical time. If the pup's early behavior is well managed, he or she will never learn to chew the furniture, climb on the counters, and urinate in the back bedroom. Through the judicious use of pens or crates, fenced yards, adult dog baby-sitters, leashes, and direct supervision when a dog first comes into your home, it is much easier to prevent unwanted behaviors than it is to unteach them.

You may want to try the "umbilical cord" approach that can be especially helpful introducing a puppy into your home. Consider keeping the pup at all times in a pen or crate, in a safely fenced and puppy-proofed yard with company, or under direct supervision in the house.

With any new arrival, it's a good idea to provide a variety of enticing chew toys. Consider stuffing the toys with cream cheese, peanut butter, freeze-dried liver, or kibble. Getting the food out of these toys will keep your pet occupied while he or she is adjusting to the new home.

The Routine

Getting your dog into a routine is important. With a puppy, you might consider a wake-up call for elimination at 5:30 a.m., then breakfast back inside the pen or crate where the dog sleeps. Structure a day that consists of lots of trips in and out, interspersed with three meals and several short training sessions. Within two days, the puppy may be galloping into the pen at the "Go to your pen" cue, ready to eat. You also can work on some simple behavior modification by ignoring unwanted behavior, such as the dog jumping up on people, and rewarding with treats for positive behavior, such as sitting.

Housetraining and crate-training

Start your dog's housetraining on Day One, teaching a verbal cue that accompanies elimination, and providing a reward to help link the two. Take the dog outside on a leash. As he or she begins to urinate, use your verbal command, then follow it with a treat and a "Click!" if you have chosen to adopt the clicker training method described elsewhere in this book. A puppy will need to go out every two hours during the day in the first weeks in your home, providing lots of opportunities for him or her to become housetrained without an accident in the house.

It's important to accompany the puppy outside during housetraining. If the dog goes outside alone, he or she may not eliminate at all, especially if returning inside results in a treat. If coming in is the behavior that gets rewarded with a treat, your dog may well decide to skip the very reason he or she has been sent outside!

It's also important to reward the dog immediately after elimination so that the linkage is made. Using the "Click!" from a clicker provides a clear message about which behavior is getting rewarded, even if the treat arrives a few seconds later.

Afterward, lead the pup back into the room where the crate is, and toss a treat into it. If it's time for a nap or for the dog to settle down for the night, give your "Go to bed" command and gently close the door as the pup noses around looking for the treat. The dog may cry for a few minutes the first few times, but if the pup is ignored, he or she will eventually curl up and learn to sleep without complaining.

When it's time for the pup to be released, turn away if he or she jumps up when you approach the crate. Wait for the puppy to sit quietly before you proceed. The dog will quickly learn that the sooner he or she sits and stays sitting, the sooner the gate opens. If he or she gets up before being released, the gate is closed again. Soon, you won't even have to ask the dog to sit; that will happen automatically because sitting gets the puppy what he or she wants—out! You're helping your dog learn without being nagged or scolded how to do the right thing.

This is a key element of positive reinforcement training—teaching the dog to take responsibility for his own behavior rather than always being told what to do.

Bite

Puppies separated too early from their litter in particular can be excessively mouthy. They didn't have the opportunity to learn from play with their littermates when a bite is too hard. If this is the case with your puppy, it's important to teach him or her to soften the uninhibited bite. Offer a treat in a closed fist; as the puppy's bite softens, give verbal cues: "Gentle," then "Click!," then, "Take it!" and the treat is given. It may take a few weeks, but the puppy will learn a gentle mouth is required to get a treat.

A Constant Watchful Eye

If your new arrival is free inside the house, direct supervision is required. There are plenty of things for the two of you to work on. Try teaching the "Down" command, at first providing a reward just for the down. Gradually increase the amount of time between the "Down" and the treat. ("Gradually" means a few seconds at a time!)

When you go outside to pick up the morning newspaper, take the dog along on a leash. Provide rewards when the dog walks with you; if he or she pulls on the leash, employ a "stop and stand still." The dog soon will learn that pulling does not get rewarded—and actually slows down the trip.

Only the Beginning

Does this process sound exhausting? Well, it does take work to get your dog off to the right start. But there is an inherent satisfaction in shaping a dog's behavior, watching him or her explore the world and teaching the animal to be a good canine citizen. ■

4

The First Command: "Come, Now"

Rewards, clarity and repetition are the keys to training your dog to come— every time you call.

"Come" is probably the most basic command every dog needs to learn. A dog who won't come when called is a danger to himself or herself and others and a headache for his or her owner.

We've all been there: standing hopelessly on the back steps calling and calling our dog, only to be ignored. Letting the dog off the leash to play and then discovering that part of the game is staying away as long as possible.

The "Come" command is fundamental to all dog training. With this command, you establish your authority, teach your dog to respect you and, of course, keep the animal out of harm's way. But let's be realistic about this. Even though your dog needs to learn you're the authority figure, no dog will run to a human if he has experienced something unpleasant as a result of obeying the command. To get your dog to come to you every time, you have to make it worth his or her while.

"Come" needs to be the sweetest word your dog ever hears; it should always mean rewards, including praise. Never, ever call your dog to you if something the animal considers unpleasant—like a bath, nail trimming or any sort of punishment. "Come" must always mean that something good will happen to your dog. If something the dog considers unpleasant is going to happen, go to him or her; don't use "Come." That word should always mean joy, love, hugs and treats, never punishment or unpleasantness.

First Step: Get Your Dog's Attention

Before you can start teaching your dog to come on command, you must first get his or her attention. Often, this is more difficult than it sounds. Until the command is understood, don't call your dog when he or she is busy checking out something more interesting than you. And, use the dog's name only when you want his attention—never because he or she is in trouble.

It's pretty easy to get a puppy's attention: just rattle the food dish. After the pup responds to that familiar sound a few times, start saying "Come," followed by his or her name. Your puppy soon will begin responding and will associate all three cues. Then, when you're certain the pup recognizes his or her name, find a time the animal is roaming aimlessly looking for something to do, then call him or her. If you get a response, you're off to a successful start.

The human voice is a very effective tool when training a dog. Learn to cultivate yours. Try not to sound angry when you are delighted with your dog. The actual words you use mean nothing— the tone is all important. Even if you're angry, use your normal calling voice. Otherwise your dog will know there's trouble and the old "fight or flight" response will kick in.

Later on when you are training your dog to walk properly on a

lead, get his or her attention by using the animal's name. Granted, getting and keeping a dog's attention can be two entirely different things. Small puppies cannot pay attention to anything for very long, so be prepared to accept just a few seconds at first.

As your pup grows older, his or her concentration ability will grow as well. Err on the side of caution; don't try to keep the dog's attention for a second longer than his or her limit.

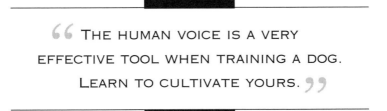

> 66 THE HUMAN VOICE IS A VERY
> EFFECTIVE TOOL WHEN TRAINING A DOG.
> LEARN TO CULTIVATE YOURS. 99

Come!

Dogs respond to cues. In the case of an oral command, when your dog responds, he or she is reacting to a memorable sound.

As with all dog training skills, find one command for the desired action and stick with it. Obviously, if you want your dog to come, "Come" is a natural. The hard "K" sound is easy for the dog to hear and understand. If you prefer "Here" or any other word, then by all means use it.

Be consistent. If you yell "Come here boy," one time, and "Here, boy," the next, it can be confusing. Your dog must be able to figure out what you want, and if there's confusion you won't get the correct response. Extra words are superfluous; if "Come" is mixed in with other sounds, your dog may miss the command entirely.

Treats and Tricks

Food, used carefully, is a great motivator for dogs, especially pups. But make your dog earn those treats. Some people think that it is good enough just to throw food at a dog. It isn't. It must have a meaning for the dog or it is wasted.

Toys are also good, especially if your dog isn't motivated by treats or if you're worried about your dog's weight. Have a special toy that the dog likes and keep it only for training sessions. Produce the toy and, if you get the dog's full attention for a second or two, break off and play. Try for another second the next time and gradually build up. Don't ever be so predictable that your dog knows exactly what you are going to do next. You want the animal's full attention; otherwise, you are wasting your time.

Play with your dog as much as you can so that your time together is the best thing that happens to him or her, and you'll receive the animal's complete attention. In essence, you'll become the ultimate toy.

But the dog also needs to know when you're serious. Serious doesn't mean threatening; otherwise, you'll see a "fight or flight" reaction. Only when you have that level of understanding can any serious training begin.

Who's in Charge?

Dogs understand pecking order. You're the boss, and the sooner your dog learns that in your relationship the better. To achieve this, it's recommended that you work with your dog every day.

Begin with a short lead attached to the dog's collar. Move a few feet away and say, "Come." If the dog obeys, offer praise and a treat. If the dog doesn't come, give a tug on the lead. When the dog does come, even if it takes a while, provide a treat and praise; don't give a scolding. Once you're sure the dog understands the command, allow for more slack in the lead and do it again. Then more slack. Do not allow detours en route. Once you're sure the animal fully understands and can be trusted, let your dog off the lead and then call "Come" from a few feet away.

Throughout the day, stop what you're doing for a minute and call your dog. Reward profusely for obedience. Do this whether the dog is three feet away or in a different part of the house. Practice often and make coming when called the most enjoyable thing in your dog's life.

Be patient. Don't expect your dog to get it right away. Most trainers believe you shouldn't feel confident that your dog will come immediately, every time, under any circumstances and in any place until you have repeated the command at least tens of thousands of times. Even then, remember, training only increases the probability of a correct response; there is no perfection. When a dog makes a mistake, try to be positive in your response. Treat it as a benefit to the training process, an additional opportunity for communication between you and your pet.

> " DOGS UNDERSTAND PECKING ORDER.
> YOU'RE THE BOSS, AND THE SOONER
> YOUR DOG LEARNS THAT IN YOUR
> RELATIONSHIP THE BETTER. "

Praise

Up to this point we've encouraged rewarding your dog. The animal comes when called and gets a treat. This raises the possibility of your dog connecting the stimulus ("Come") and the response ("Coming"). Ultimately, praise should be enough. Once you're sure the dog fully understands and comes every time, begin reducing the treats. After all, the goal is to get the dog to do what he or she is told. Still, people always feel the need to quit using food for training long before they should. Eventually you'll need to: you don't always have food to give, but your praise will always be there.

It takes a good deal longer to train effectively than most people think, so don't be in a hurry to drop the treats until you're sure they are no longer necessary.

Lying Down on the Job

As you doubtless know by now, your dog has boundless energy. That energy also means he or she can probably outlast you. If your dog knows you'll yell "Come" three times before you come after him or her, the animal will wait for the third time (or five or six) before responding. Why? Because that's the way you taught the command. If you want the dog to come the first time you call, teach that. Start when you're working together with the lead. Call once; if the dog doesn't come, give the lead a tug.

If you know your dog understands the command to come but does not respond, don't waste time calling his or her name over and over. The dog will learn that it's okay to ignore you.

Instead, get your leash. Call the dog again, using a happy, encouraging voice but only give the command just once. If there's no response, go get the dog. Don't scold or punish; just snap on the leash and go straight to the house. No punishment—but no rewards either.

Scolding

Sometimes, a dog needs to be punished. Since not all dogs are the same, there are those who need a firmer hand. Since words themselves are irrelevant, let your tone of voice do the scolding.

Remember—don't call the dog to come so that you can scold. Go to the animal. Don't worry that your dog won't like you if you scold him or her. If a dog is treated with love, the love in return is practically unconditional. In fact, the more the dog respects you, the more intense the bond between you and your dog.

Playing and Training by Tugging

From tiny Pomeranians to huge Mastiffs, dogs love to play tug-of-war. There is something in growling, grabbing, pulling, shaking, ripping and shredding that satisfies a dog's basic predatory instincts. Owners also find it rewarding to roughhouse with their four-footed friends, and tug-of-war is a great way to take the edge off a high-energy dog.

Many trainers caution against playing such games, warning that they teach dogs to be dominant and aggressive. However, if you play the game right, it's a perfect opportunity to teach your dog deference and good manners and you can even resolve aggression problems. Only if it is done improperly does tug-of-war teach your dog bad habits.

The first key is that you always win, especially in the beginning. The game toy should be a very special, cherished object. Keep it hidden in a special place, and bring it out only when you want to play. Tease your dog with the toy; shake it a squeak it, and use a word such as "tug" or "pull" as your behavior cue. Let your dog grab one end, and have a great time tugging and shaking the toy together for a few minutes, then offer a very tasty treat.

If you've used a sufficiently tasty treat, your dog will open his mouth for it. When that happens, say "Drop," or "Give," since to get the treat, the toy must be dropped. You just won the game. "Click!" a clicker or tell the dog "Yes!" to so the animal understands he or she did a rewardable behavior, then hold the treat for canine nibbling while you safely remove the tug toy. Now you can either play again (playing the game again is another reward for giving up the toy when you asked) or put it away and play again later.

Before long, your dog will be programmed to drop the toy on cue, and you can win whenever you want. Now you can let him or her grab it and run off with it every once in a while to make the game more interesting. Just remember to you should always end up with the toy— don't start playing chase!

Some dogs want to play too aggressively with a tug toy, and some dogs get seriously aggressive. If your dog plays too rough, and jumps up on you or puts his or her mouth on your clothing or skin, it's time for an instant "time out!" Just say "Too bad!" in an upbeat, cheerful, non-punitive tone of voice and put the toy away for a few minutes. If the rowdy behavior persists, use a tie-down, a crate or a puppy pen, or just step out of the room briefly. After a moment or two, resume the game. Every time the dog nips or gets out of control, give as "Too bad!" and a time-out. Four time-outs in a row end the game for the day. Your dog will learn quickly that too much roughness ends playtime,and he or she will begin to control the behavior so that the game can continue. ■

5

Click!

*The secret to effectively training your
dog may be only a click away.*

T he concept is so simple: use a consistent command and a
novel sound to link positive behavior and a reward to teach
your dog what you want from him or her. Simple, yes, but
as is the case with many simple things, it works. Many dog
owners and trainers swear by clicker training. This method can be
easy for the average dog owner to use because it does not require a
lot of practice and skill; it only requires an open mind.

Clicker Training: Fun, Fast, Flexible

Clicker training is an informal term that many trainers use for "applied operant conditioning," that is, **training with positive reinforcement**, wherein the clicker trainer uses treats to reward the
animal for a desired behavior.

The click! sound serves as a **marker signal**, or **bridge**, that provides instant feedback rewarding desired behavior. The dog quickly learns what behavior produced the treat and to reproduce that
behavior for additional rewards.

There is an art to knowing how to time the click!, the verbal cue,
and the reward. Done properly, clicker training communicates the
"good dog" message quickly and clearly when your dog does what
you want.

Making Noise
Most people use a plastic-and-metal thumb clicker, but any noisemaker (such as a standard ballpoint pen) that can make a consis-

tently audible sound will do. The sound needs to be distinct enough that your dog will be able to differentiate it from other sounds he or she hears regularly.

―――――――――

" The Click! sound serves as a marker signal, or bridge, that gives the animal instant feedback about what behavior is desired. "

―――――――――

Once you've got a suitable noisemaker, click the clicker precisely when your dog does something you like and follow up quickly with a tantalizing food treat so the dog associates the sound with yummy reinforcement. Treats should be small but potent—a savory morsel your dog adores rather than his or her regular kibble or a run-of-the-mill dog biscuit.

The timing of the click in relation to the desired behavior is crucial. "If more than a half-second elapses between the behavior and the click, you will inadvertently reward behavior that happens after the behavior you want," notes Dr. Gerry Flannigan, a North Carolina veterinarian.

Once your dog understands the basic click-and-treat scenario, introduce a target stick (a dowel or yardstick) as the foundation for eliciting specific behaviors. Hold the target stick in front of your dog and click as soon as the dog touches the stick with his or her nose—which most dogs do naturally out of curiosity.

Steps to Success

Break "big picture" behavior into smaller tasks. Once your dog has a small behavior down pat, such as touching the target stick with his or her nose, use that success as the springboard for training a different but related behavior, such as touching the stick with a paw.

When your dog reliably performs a certain behavior, add a vocal cue such as "high five," then click and treat only behavior that obeys that vocal cue. Never correct, reprimand, or punish a dog who doesn't heed the cue. Simply don't click and treat. "The opposite of reward is not punishment; it's no reward," explains Dr. Flannigan.

To teach a new behavior, you have to click and treat every time it occurs. But once your dog knows the behavior, click and treat only intermittently and randomly. Sporadic rewards keep the dog enthusiastic about "playing the game."

One of the beauties of clicker training is that it engages the dog's mind. "Clicker training is about getting the dog to think, 'What can I do to get this person to click?'" says Karen Pryor, a trainer and author of the book *Don't Shoot the Dog*. "It's not a rigid technique, and it's fun for both people and dogs."

Principles of Operant Conditioning

Clicker training is based on the principles of operant conditioning. Those principles include the existence of a **stimulus** (in this case, any change to the environment to which your dog can respond or react); **reinforcement**, the strengthening a response to a stimulus; and **extinction**, the weakening of a response to a stimulus through non-reinforcement.

When we train through positive reinforcement, we reinforce behaviors by marking (clicking) the ones we want, and extinguish the behaviors we don't want by ignoring them (non-reinforcement) rather than punishing them.

A dog who tries to get attention or food by barking will quickly learn that barking is counterproductive if you turn your back when the barking starts. If you are consistent in your response, the barking will eventually extinguish. He or she will learn this lesson even more quickly if you click! and provide a reward when the barking has stopped. Gradually extend the length of time you expect your dog to stay quiet before clicking and rewarding. Many owners inadvertently do the exact opposite by ignoring the dog when he or she is quiet and paying attention and "shushing" the dog for barking, thus teaching that barking provides the attention that the animal craves.

ABCs of Behavior

■ *Antecedents* *are events that occur before the behavior. We can increase the dog's response to the antecedent if we make it more salient—that is, we make it stand out from the other stimuli that are present in the environment by giving it meaning. A cue, or signal, for a dog to do something is given meaning when we show him or* her that the appropriate response to the cue will be reinforced (with a treat).

■ **Behavior** means anything that the dog does, such as sit, lie down, come, bark, jump up, run away, eat, dig, howl. A response is the particular piece of behavior we are working to modify or reinforce.

■ **Consequences** are events that happen after a behavior or response takes place.

For example, if your dog sits when you say "Sit!," you provide him a piece of hot dog. The word "Sit!" is the **antecedent**, the dog's sit is the **behavior**, or response, and the piece of hot dog is the **consequence**.

The kind of training you have employed is called **operant conditioning** because the dog's response (sit) operates in the environment—that is, it has an effect on and, at least to some degree, controls the consequence.

Training Concepts

In clicker training, the timing of the reinforcement is critical. You must know and visualize exactly what kinds of behaviors you will click! and reward, or you will be late. When your reinforcement is late, you are actually rewarding the wrong behavior.

For instance, if you are trying to teach your dog to retrieve, you might begin by clicking and providing a reward each time the dog touches his or her nose to a ball. You must click! the instant the nose touches the ball, and follow the click with a treat. If you are late with the click! you will be providing reinforcement for moving away from the ball rather than for touching it. While an occasional late click! is not critical, routinely clicking too late can prevent your dog from learning to fetch the ball.

Make sure the animal thoroughly grasps each step before proceeding to the next. Don't go too quickly; just because you understand the point doesn't mean your dog does.

For example, when your dog suddenly seems to lose the concept of the behavior you are trying to train, it is a sign that you may have taken too big a step forward. Step back to the last place the dog was doing well, reinforce the behavior there, and figure out how to break the next step down into smaller increments.

Let's say you have succeeded in getting your dog to reliably pick up the ball on cue. In your excitement over your success, you now toss the ball across the yard and give the dog the cue to pick it up. The dog stands and looks at you uncomprehendingly. You have taken too big a step.

If the dog has been picking up the ball from the ground directly in front of him or her, go back and repeat and reinforce this response a few times. Now you might try moving the ball just a foot away and giving the cue. If that is too much, you might try six inches, or three, until the dog is consistently responding the way you want, and then continue increasing the distance in small increments, until he or she will fetch the ball from across the yard.

To avoid making the mistake of going too fast, analyze the topography, or shape, of the behavior before you begin to train a new behavior. Then, create a written training plan and lay out the goals for each session. While you may have a goal in mind for each session, you must also be flexible and be prepared to revise the plan if it isn't working, by re-analyzing the behavior and looking for different ways to approach the training, perhaps breaking down the steps into even smaller increments.

A Little Clicker Training History

The use of operant conditioning in animal training goes back to the 1940s, when Marian and Keller Breland founded Animal Behavior Enterprises. The Brelands worked with behaviorist B. F. Skinner during World War II, training pigeons to guide missiles. They also created training programs and manuals for dolphin trainers— methods still in use today.

The couple began working with Bob Bailey, who in 1964 was the first person to make a successful release and recovery at sea of a trained dolphin. Following Keller's death in 1965, Marie and Bob continued to work together, and eventually married. The three trainers have trained more than 140 different species of animals using Skinner's principles of operant conditioning and the techniques they developed. Marie died in 2001; Bob still offers operant conditioning and behavior analysis workshops, primarily in his home base of Hot Springs,

*Arkansas. For more information, see **www.hsnp.com/behavior.***

Clicker training became more widely known in the dog world in the 1980s with trainer Karen Pryor's book, Don't Shoot the Dog. *A revised edition was published in 1999. For more information about Karen, see **www.clickertraining.com**.*

Reinforce, Reinforce!

A key concept to successful clicker training and successful training in general is giving lots of reinforcement. Many dog owners and trainers are too stingy with the click! and reward. If you don't give enough reinforcement, you lose your dog's attention. And, don't stop providing rewards too soon. Remember that praise and petting are also rewards; food isn't always necessary.

Responding to your requests for behavior is your dog's job, so make sure you "pay" him or her for doing it. Most people wouldn't continue working unless they got paid. Why should our dogs work for free? ■

6

Your Dog and the Law

*Just as motorists can be held liable for
damage they do with their cars, dog owners
can be held liable for harm done by their dogs.*

D ogs and people have lived in relative harmony for thousands of years. But as population growth brings both species physically closer, an ever-growing body of "dog law" is emerging intended to strengthen, not threaten, the institution of dog ownership. They safeguard an individual's right to own a dog while also assuring the public's health and safety.

"Think of dog-related laws as opportunities to protect the public, yourself, and your dog," advises Jerrold Tannenbaum, an attorney, ethicist, and professor of veterinary medicine at the University of California, Davis. Knowing—and abiding by—your state and local dog laws will help you avoid disputes with neighbors and unpleasant encounters with the legal system.

Dogs as Property

Legally speaking, pet dogs are domestic animals. As such, the law considers them the property of their owners. (Wild animals, on the other hand, are technically the property of the state, unless the state gives private citizens permission to own them.) But the law attaches certain conditions and obligations to the privilege of owning a dog, just as it does to the privilege of owning and driving a car. Just as motorists can be held liable for damage they do with their cars, dog owners can be held liable for harm done by their dogs.

Liability

Your state's liability law for damage or injury caused by dogs can rely on two quite different tests: negligence (the failure to act as a reasonable and prudent person would act under the given circumstances) and strict liability (automatic liability regardless of fault). In all states, negligent owners can be held liable for harm done by their dogs. And a growing number of states impose strict liability on owners for dog-related injury and damage.

No matter which state criterion applies, your local government probably wields a good deal of authority over animal-control issues. Although the U.S. Constitution prohibits the government from seizing property (including dogs) without notification and the opportunity to be heard, "states and localities have enormous leeway in determining exactly what the notice and the opportunity to be heard will be," Tannenbaum says. Consequently, many dogs suffer impoundment (capture and confinement) while people untangle the legal knots.

Strict-liability laws dictate that an owner is liable for injury (and, in some states, damage) caused by his or her dog regardless of whether the owner is negligent. Some strict-liability statutes, however, do not impose liability for dog-caused injury to trespassers or to anyone who has taunted or provoked the animal. But because mail carriers and delivery people have an "implied invitation" to be on your premises, technically they are not trespassing. Also, most states do not view a child who wanders uninvited onto your property as a trespasser.

The rule of negligence says that owners are responsible for injury or damage if they knew, or if a reasonable person should have known, that the dog would do harm under the given circumstances. Some mistakenly call this the "one-bite" rule, thinking—incorrectly—that the law gives each dog owner one "free bite." The one-bite fallacy is based on the discredited theory that an owner cannot possibly know that a dog is dangerous until the animal has actually bitten someone. In fact, a dog's growling or teeth baring could be a precursor to more harmful forms of aggression and should put the owner on notice.

To understand the difference between the two liability theories, consider this scenario: your friend, who has known and played with your always affectionate pooch for years, is visiting at your invitation. Without warning, the dog bites your friend's leg. Under strict liability, you are liable even though you had no reason to know your dog might bite and therefore no reason to take precautions.

But under the negligence rule, you would not be legally responsible for failing to protect your friend. You did not know—nor could you have known—that the dog would bite, and therefore, you would not be found negligent. (Common courtesy, however, might impel you to reimburse your friend's medical expenses.)

Note also that in some jurisdictions, anyone harboring a dog is considered legally responsible for damage done by the dog. And if you care for a stray (an apparently unowned dog), you might be responsible for the consequences of the dog's behavior while the animal is under your care, even if the legal owner eventually turns up.

> 66 DOG OWNERS SHOULD HAVE SUFFICIENT
> LIABILITY COVERAGE TO TAKE CARE OF ANY
> CONCEIVABLE DAMAGE... 99

Insurance to the Rescue?

The good news is that should your dog trample the neighbor's prized petunias, your homeowner's or renter's insurance policy probably covers dog-created damage, regardless of fault. Review your insurance policy and call your agent if the legal jargon confuses you. Most homeowner policies offer liability coverage from $100,000 to $300,000. "Dog owners should have sufficient liability coverage to take care of any conceivable damage," advises Tannenbaum.

The not-so-good news is that many insurance companies invoke their own "one-bite" rule. After the first dog-bite claim, they may cancel the insurance or exclude dog-related incidents from the coverage. Owners of "problem" dogs may therefore have to pay high rates to specialty insurance companies to cover dog liability.

Even with insurance protection, you're still better off spending the time to raise a well-mannered dog than winding up in a legal dispute because you've ignored the basics of good canine citizenship. Visit your town hall or contact a local dog club to learn what laws are on the books about dogs. Find out if your state applies strict liability or less stringent criteria.

Licensing & Vaccinations

Most states and local governments require licensing of dogs. License records help reunite lost dogs with their owners—which only works if your dog wears his or her license tag. Most courts have ruled that if a dog is unlicensed (as untagged dogs often are assumed to be) and running at large (roaming freely and not under a person's control), the local government has the power to impound the dog.

Licensing also helps the state keep track of vaccination histories. Almost all states require vaccination of dogs older than four to six months. Most cities and towns require proof of rabies vaccination before they will license your dog. Some cities also require proof of distemper vaccination. But these are only minimum legal requirements. Your veterinarian may recommend further vaccination protection. Also, because laws vary from state to state, it's wise to carry vaccination records when traveling with your dog.

Canine Good Citizenship

Dog-related legal problems usually arise because owners fail to adequately restrain or train their dogs. Here's how to avoid run-ins with your neighbors or local officials:

■ *Never let your dog run at large.*

■ *Keep your dog's license and vaccinations current.*

■ *Closely supervise your dog among strangers and children—both on and off your property.*

■ *Train your dog in basic obedience and quickly remedy behavioral problems.*

■ *Curb excessive barking. If your dog interferes with the neighbors' enjoyment of their property, you could find yourself facing a nuisance complaint.*

Leash Laws

Most densely populated municipalities have dog restraint laws. The language of these laws varies, but they generally require that a dog be on a leash and under control when not on the owner's premises. In most leash-law-governed communities, animal control officials can automatically impound dogs running at large—even if they are licensed and tagged. In rural areas of several states, animal control officials (and, sometimes, landowners) can legally kill your dog if the animal is attacking or "worrying" livestock. Therefore, dog owners living anywhere near livestock should never let their dogs run loose.

If your town has a leash law and your dog damages property or causes personal injury while at large, you probably will be considered negligent and therefore responsible for making restitution. Even if your community does not have a leash law, you may still be held liable under state law for damage or injury your dog causes.

Public Health

Some cities, concerned about health risks posed by large concentrations of dogs, limit the number of dogs per household. Despite challenges to such laws, Tannenbaum says that "the courts have been virtually unanimous in ruling that the government has the right to protect the public peace, health, and safety by enacting such laws."

Urban and suburban dogs often have no choice but to eliminate in public. In response, many heavily populated communities have passed so-called "pooper-scooper" laws as a public health measure. Even the most ardent dog lover who has stepped in publicly deposited dog droppings appreciates the value of these ordinances.

Handling Disputes

What can you do if the dog whose barking is driving you insane is not your dog? Probably the most common complaint about dogs is the noise they make. The good news for neighbors is that usually problems can be resolved without resorting to legal means, through informal negotiation or mediation. And if that fails, there is almost always a law against noisy nuisance dogs.

If you can't get these laws enforced to your satisfaction, you can sue the dog owner to get the nuisance stopped and to recover money damages. But substituting a major hassle with expensive lawyers for a small one with a bad-mannered spaniel isn't much progress. Lawsuits are especially undesirable when the other party is a neighbor—after all, you'll still be next door to each other no matter who wins.

Here are some ways to resolve dog disputes out of court and stay on relatively good terms with the neighbors.

Talking to Your Neighbor

The obvious first step—asking the dog's owner to stop the noise—is either ignored or botched by a surprising number of people, probably because approaching someone with a complaint can be unpleasant and even intimidating.

However, talking to your neighbor calmly and reasonably is essential. Even if you do eventually end up in court, a judge isn't likely to be too sympathetic if you didn't make at least some effort to work things out first. If you approach the situation with a modicum of tact, you may be pleasantly surprised with the result.

Sometimes owners are blissfully unaware that there's a problem. If a dog barks for hours every day—but only when he or she is left alone—the owner may not know that a neighbor is being driven crazy. Even if you're sure the neighbor does know about the dog's behavior, it may be better to proceed as though she doesn't.

Getting the Most From Negotiating

- ■ *Write a friendly note or call to arrange a convenient time to talk. Don't blunder up some rainy evening when the neighbor is trying to drag groceries and kids into the house after work.*

- ■ *If you think it's appropriate, take a little something to the meeting to break the ice—some vegetables from your garden, perhaps.*

- ■ *Don't threaten legal action (or worse, illegal action). There will be time to discuss legal remedies if relations deteriorate.*

- ■ *Offer positive suggestions. Once you have established some rapport, you may want to suggest, tactfully, that the owner get help with the dog. Try saying something like, "You know, my friend Tom had the same problem with his dog, and since he's been taking the dog to ABC Obedience School classes, he and his neighbors are much happier." Of course, if you make suggestions too early in the process, the neighbor may resent your "interference."*

■ *Try to agree on specific actions to alleviate the problem: for example, that the dog is kept inside between 10 p.m. and 8 a.m.*

■ *After you agree on a plan, set a date to talk again in a couple of weeks. If your next meeting is already arranged, it will be easier for you to talk again. It won't look like you're badgering your neighbor, but will show that you're serious about getting the problem solved.*

■ *If the situation improves, make a point to say thanks. Not only is it the nice thing to do, it will also encourage more progress.*

Mediation: Getting Another Person to Help

If talking to your neighbor directly doesn't work or you're convinced it's hopeless, consider getting some help from a mediator. A mediator won't make a decision for you, but will help you and your neighbor agree on a way to resolve the problem.

Mediators, both professionals and volunteers, are trained to listen to both sides, identify problems, keep everyone focused on the real problems, and suggest compromises. Going through the process helps both people feel they've been heard (a more constructive version of the satisfaction of "having your day in court") and often puts people on better terms.

Mediation provides a safe, structured way for neighbors to talk. They meet informally with one or more mediators, and first agree on ground rules—basic guidelines, such as no name-calling or interrupting. Then, each person briefly states a view of the problem. The mediator may summarize the problem and its history before moving on to discuss possible solutions.

Unlike a lawsuit, mediation is not an adversarial process. You do not go to mediation to argue your side. No judge makes a decision for you. People can become amazingly cooperative when they realize they are empowered to resolve their own problem.

When two people do agree on how to alleviate the problem, it's best to put the agreement in writing, which helps clarify everyone's expectations. And it's invaluable if memories grow fuzzy later, as they almost always do, about who agreed to do what.

The best place to look for a free mediator for this kind of dispute is a community mediation group. Many cities have such groups. Other places that may be able to refer you to a mediation service include the small claims court clerk's office, the local district attorney's office, radio or television stations that offer help with consumer problems, or state or local bar associations.

Dangerous-Dog Laws

The question of how to deal with dogs who bite or attack is highly provocative. Ordinances that stipulate conditions for owning—and punishing—dogs deemed "dangerous" or "vicious" inevitably provoke controversy. Local and state laws banning or severely restricting ownership of specific breeds have incited the most debate.

Many municipalities have dangerous-dog ordinances target specific breeds. But such laws often fail to assign responsibility where it really lies. "It doesn't make sense to blame the dog for what it has done when the real problem is the owner," says Andrew Rowan, an executive with the Humane Society of the United States. Such laws attribute viciousness to bloodlines alone, ignoring the fact that dogs can learn aggressive behavior from—or have it reinforced by—irresponsible, careless owners. These laws also discriminate against responsible owners of targeted breeds who raise upstanding canine citizens by carefully training and properly socializing their dogs.

Moreover, breed-specific ordinances can backfire. Many cities that outlawed or restricted pit bull ownership in the late 1980s saw the population of other potentially pugnacious breeds soar. (And, occasionally, dogs that merely looked like members of a restricted or banned breed were victimized.) "Breed-specific restrictions don't change the total number of dogs capable of administering a nasty bite," Rowan says. "All such regulations do is change the local breed distribution." Having realized these short-comings, dozens of communities that once considered or enacted breed-specific ordinances now have more general regulations.

Among the most progressive localities is Multnomah County, Oregon. In 1986, the county enacted an ordinance that strikes the delicate balance between public safety and the rights of responsible dog owners. Multnomah's system, developed by a task force of animal-control personnel, dog club representatives, public health officials, and veterinarians, places offending dogs (regardless of breed)—and their owners—in one of four categories. The more serious the infraction, the stiffer the restrictions, which range from physically confining the dog and requiring the owner to pass a responsible pet-ownership test to euthanizing the dog and suspending the owner's right to keep dogs.

Multnomah's classification scheme works. In the first three years, the number of repeat biting or attacking incidents fell from 25 to 7 percent. Consistent enforcement and precise record-keeping also contribute to the system's success. "If Multnomah County-type programs were instituted nationwide, I think the incidence of dog bites—certainly serious dog bites—would drop dramatically," Rowan says.

State and Local Laws

If the situation doesn't improve after your efforts, it's time to check your local laws and explore your legal options. Armed with this knowledge, you'll be better prepared to approach your neighbor again or go to animal control authorities, the police, or a small claims court.

In some places, barking dogs are covered by a specific law or ordinance. If there's no law aimed specifically at dogs, a general nuisance or noise ordinance will make the owner responsible. Local law may forbid loud noise after 10 p.m., for example, or prohibit any "unreasonable" noise. And someone who allows a dog to bark after numerous warnings from police may be arrested for disturbing the peace.

To find out what the law is where you live, go to a law library and check the state statutes and city or county ordinances. Look in the index under "noise," "dogs," "animals" or "nuisance." If you don't have access to a law library, you can probably find out about local laws by calling the local animal control agency or city attorney.

Animal Control Authorities

If your efforts at working something out with your neighbor haven't succeeded, talk to the animal control department in your city or county. The people there are likely to be more receptive than the police or other municipal officials.

When you call, don't just make your complaint and hang up. If it's really a persistent problem, you need to be persistent, too. Ask the person you talk to—and write down his or her name, so you won't have to explain your problem every time you call—about the department's procedures. Find out what the department will do, and when. For example, the department may need to receive a certain number of complaints about a barking dog within a certain time before it will act.

Police

The police aren't very interested in barking dog problems, and you can't much blame them. Unless you live in an exceptionally quiet and peaceful place, they have more serious problems on their hands.

Another reason to avoid the police, except as a last resort, is that summoning a cruiser to a neighbor's house obviously will not improve your already strained relations. But if none of the options already discussed works, and the relationship with your neighbor is shot anyway, you might as well give the police a try.

The police have the power to enforce local noise laws and laws that prohibit disturbing the peace. As when you're dealing with animal control people, don't be afraid to ask the police exactly what

German shepherds are among the breeds named in many dangerous-dog ordinances. Such ordinances fail to recognize that viciousness more often results from a lack of training—or irresponsible training—than from bloodlines.

you and other neighbors must do to get them to take action. You may well have to make more than one call or written complaint.

Small Claims Court

If nothing you've tried helps, you can sue the owner of a barking dog on the grounds that the dog is a nuisance interfering with your use and enjoyment of your home. The least painful route is through small claims court. Small claims court procedures are simple and are designed to be used without a lawyer. In some states, including California, lawyers are barred from small claims court. Even if they aren't banned, you will rarely see one there because most people find it too expensive to hire them. Fees in small claims court are also low, and the process is relatively fast—which means you'll get to court in a few weeks or months, not years.

Winning a lawsuit in small claims court can get you money (and satisfaction), but probably nothing else. In most states, small claims court judges only have the power to order someone to pay money. They can't give you what you really want—a court order telling your neighbor to make the problematic dog be quiet.

Still, making your neighbor fork over some money may be even more effective than a simple court order in convincing your neighbor to clean up his or her (or the dog's) act. And you can keep going back to court and asking for more as long as the nuisance continues.

If you absolutely must have a court order telling the neighbor to stop (the technical term for this kind of order is an injunction), you may have to go to "regular" court (often called circuit, superior or district court) instead of small claims court. For that, you'll probably need a lawyer, though you can bring a straightforward nuisance suit yourself, if you're willing to spend some hours in the law library finding out how to draw up the papers and submit them to the court.

In any neighborhood dispute, it's always best to to try to resolve things without involving outside authorities. Think about it: if your dog is creating a disturbance while you're gone, wouldn't you rather hear about it from the people next door than through the police or a legal proceeding? And if a neighbor does come to you with a complaint about your dog, be sensitive to the complaint and try to come up with a solution that keeps everyone, including your dog, happy. ■

Section II

Problem-Specific Training

7

Teaching Social Skills to Difficult Dogs

Impending aggression: how to recognize it and how to head it off—before it becomes an out-of-control problem.

Dogs fight other dogs for many reasons. They fight in aggressive play. They squabble over food and toys. They challenge each other for the best spot in the pack or the best spot on the bed. They fight to protect their puppies and other canine pack members, or to defend territory and their humans. Some fight because they've been bred or taught to fight. And a surprising number of dogs fight just because they are poorly socialized; they've never learned to speak "dog" and as canine social "nerds," they inadvertently display body language that triggers aggressive responses from other dogs. Serious dog-on-dog aggression is a common problem, and one that is often overlooked and too often tolerated. However, it is not normal dog behavior, and, in many cases, it can be prevented or mitigated.

All dogs are capable of turning on one of their canine acquaintances with a short but ferocious attack. If this happens only occasionally, these brief though dramatic interchanges are actually normal—a device dogs use to set boundaries regarding the kind of behavior they won't tolerate or to establish dominance over each other. But dogs who frequently attack other dogs without regard to the victim's behavior can cause owners a lot of trouble, heartache, and even lawsuits.

A tiny percentage of these canine bullies are born, not made; certain breeds were developed to fight each other. But far more dog-aggressive dogs are made that way by their owners—through a lack of proper socialization, inappropriate human intervention in normal canine interactions, even encouragement of aggressive behavior. In other cases, a dog slowly develops increasingly aggressive behavior that goes unchecked or unnoticed by his owner—at least until it gets bad enough that the dog seriously injures someone else's dog.

It's very frustrating for social, responsible dog owners when they end up with a dog who can't get along with other dogs. Understandably, few people want to walk with them. The walks they do take are fraught with tension, as they try to control their dog and warn other owners to keep their distance. Eventually, many people tire of the stress, and dominant canine bullies end up exiled to backyards or even put to death.

Regaining Control

Fortunately, with appropriate training, many canine social misfits can regain access to society. Some trainers offer special classes designed to teach owners new skills for dealing with their dogs' antisocial behaviors.

One goal of these classes is to teach owners how to detect and interpret their dogs' aggressive body language in time to avert confrontations with other dogs. The owners learn exercises that can distract their dogs from their aggressive focus. The owners also learn to use food lures, rewards and praise to reinforce desired behaviors.

The other major goal is to give the dogs opportunities for learning appropriate social behavior from each other. In the wild, dominant body language is most frequently used to avoid fights, since it is contrary to pack survival for dogs to go around routinely injuring each other. Most dominance moves are bluffs, designed to intimidate the opponent into bloodless submission. Occasionally, a brief scuffle ensues, rarely causing serious injury. Thus, dominance in wild packs is usually settled and maintained with relative nonviolence.

Owners of domestic dogs tend to be phobic of any display of aggression between dogs. Because of the perceived risk of serious injury to the participants, owners don't let dogs "fight it out" in an uncontrolled setting, so most dogs never experience the natural consequences of their aggressive behavior. Minor, normal, usually harmless, scuffles are often treated as major crises. The dogs are yanked apart and punished mightily. As a result, not only do the dogs not learn how to settle their squabbles peacefully, their levels of stress and aggression actually escalate.

In a class, dogs can be allowed to interact to the point of learning those consequences, with an important difference: they wear soft but strong muzzles. In this controlled setting, dogs safely get past their initial burst of aggression so they can get to the part where they learn to relate appropriately.

It's critical that dogs and owners enrolled in these classes be pre-evaluated by the trainer. Classes are custom-designed to meet the needs of the students. Protections are put in place so that big bullies are prevented from trouncing timid dogs who bite in self-defense. Where appropriate, owners can be shown some of the exercises ahead of time so their dogs get extra practice. A bully might need to spend more time practicing his or her off! exercise, while a very nervous dog might get extra homework assignments in relaxation techniques.

By the end of the course, some dogs can be fully integrated into their local canine community. Others can be given supervised freedom in a designated play group. Still others will never be trustworthy for off-leash play, but will be under much better control and far safer on-leash than they were previously.

The best results will be enjoyed by highly motivated owners who enjoy close bonds with their dogs. Dogs who are responsive and connected to their owners and who are easily motivated by food, praise, or other rewards are most likely to benefit from this type of class. Independent dogs who are oblivious to their owners' presence and behavior requests are more likely to fail.

Muzzles for Safety

For safety, some aggressive dogs should wear a muzzle. The best muzzles are soft but strong. These are comfortable for the dog, can be fitted snugly behind the dog's head, and allow enough freedom to eat treats. Muzzles should not be worn for more than fifteen to twenty minutes, since they restrict the dog's ability to pant and self-cool.

A Typical Class

Food is an important part of a successful socialization class. Instructors use positive methods to reduce the dogs' stress and to teach them that having other dogs around is a good thing. This can only be accomplished with reinforcement and reward. Food is a primary reinforcer that can be delivered quickly and easily, so its use is critical in getting a dog to think positively about a stimulus (the presence of other dogs) that has previously been perceived as a negative.

Week One

Dogs are not allowed to interact in the first session of a socialization class. Instead, certain exercises are practiced and homework is assigned so that the dogs are more responsive to their owners before the first dog-to-dog interaction in the second session. Students and their dogs spread out around the training area—with as much distance between them as possible. People and dogs are seated on blankets or rugs on the ground.

Typically, the first class features an in-depth discussion of dog behavior, aggression, and canine body language. Each owner describes his or her dog's history of aggression, and the kind of behavior he anticipates from the dog in the class setting. Owners and the instructor analyze the body language the dogs display, discuss

Relaxation Exercises How-To

1. The dog is staring intensely at a strange dog in her yard, ignoring attempts to get her attention.

2. With the use of the relax cue, gentle words and touch, the first dog begins to settle but is still conscious of the other dog.

its likely meaning, and make predictions about the dogs' behaviors during the interaction to come. It is important from the very beginning of the first class that owners begin to develop their skills in reading dog body language so they know when and how to intervene appropriately.

Next, owners discuss their feelings about their dogs and about the class. It is normal for owners to be apprehensive. It's explained that the dogs will not be allowed to hurt each other, and that one goal of the class is to allow dogs to interact safely so that they can learn appropriate body language and social behavior around each other.

Then, the work begins. Unlike regular training classes, where the instructor is upbeat, speaks cheerfully, and moves quickly, socialization classes are almost like meditation sessions. The first exercise is intended to lower the stress levels of dogs and owners with massage on a rug or blanket for the dogs, and deep breathing for the owners.

Next, dogs and owners learn an off! exercise, which means that if dogs give a hard glare to another dog, they are asked to off! and are given a click! and a treat when they look away from the other dog. They also get clicks and treats for "soft" glances (and tail wags)

3. Now she has removed her attention from the other dog and is focusing on the instructor, the massage, and the petting.

4. Now fully relaxed, the dog lies flat with her head down; her rapid panting has subsided into calm, deep breathing.

at other dogs, and lots of clicks and treats for paying attention to their owners. The purpose is to teach them that the presence of other dogs is a good thing—they get lots of treats when other dogs are around.

Another exercise that typically occurs in the first class is the "gotcha!," a positive cue (with treat reward) for a grab on a dog's collar, which becomes necessary when intervening in a scuffle.

Owners usually will practice fitting muzzles on the dogs and do one-at-a-time leash-walking around the training area. You also may be asked to practice your tone of voice (calm and upbeat, not panicked or commanding) for use with the off! cue. Relaxation exercises typically end the class, with dog and owner pairs being asked to leave calmly, one at a time, to avoid confrontations at the door.

Relaxation Exercises

Lowering the dogs' (and owners') levels of anxiety at the beginning and end of each class contributes greatly to calm behavior and positive interactions during class. It also teaches dogs and owners valuable skills to use when they find themselves in stressful situations outside of class.

Owners are taught deep breathing and voice control. They practice the verbal part of the gotcha! and off exercises (described on the following pages) without the dog present to learn to say the cue words calmly and brightly, without betraying their own anxiety. If they can control their own emotions, they can avoid heightening their dogs' stress levels.

Also recommended is teaching the dogs a verbal "Relax" cue, which includes having them lie on their sides. This is a naturally relaxing position, especially when accompanied by gentle stroking and massage.

An owner can use this anytime the dog becomes agitated by the presence of another dog—assuming the other dog is under control and will not approach or attack the dog being worked in the "relax" position.

In time, just the use of the word "relax" can elicit a conditioned response that can calm a dog at the beginning stages of arousal.

"Gotcha!"

This is a safety exercise that is beneficial for all dogs. Most dogs, at some time in their lives, will have someone grab them by the collar. Many dogs find this a frightening, threatening experience and some respond with a defensive bite.

"Gotcha!" How-To

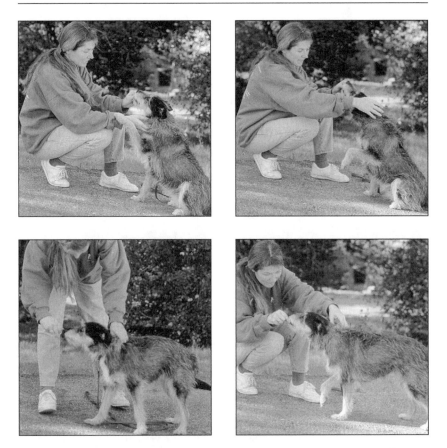

Clockwise from top left: Begin by softly saying "Gotcha!" and touching the dog's collar in the least threatening position, under the jaw, then feeding a treat. If that is too threatening, simply offer your hand with the gotcha! and feed a treat without touching. As the dog gets comfortable with the under-the-chin collar touch, repeat the exercise by circling your hand over the dog's head as you say "Gotcha!" and give a treat. If the dog tolerates that well, add the collar grasp at the back of the neck. Make sure your dog is comfortable with one phase before proceeding to the next. If he or she shrinks away from you at any point, you may have progressed too quickly. Go back to the level where the dog was comfortable and practice for a while before proceeding, more slowly this time. Practice when the dog is not looking at you and is not expecting it. If you always give a treat for the "Gotcha!", over time your dog should become more confident, not flinch from the "grab" and eagerly walk into the pressure in anticipation of the treat.

Most dogs are much more comfortable having their collars grasped under their chin rather than over their head. The back of the neck is a sensitive trigger point for dominance aggression. Train yourself to reach under, not over your dog's head to grasp the collar.

Within the context of a socialization class, teaching your dog that a collar grab is a positive thing desensitizes him or her to the movement, minimizes the likelihood of bites, and makes it safer to intervene in a class interaction.

Start this exercise (see photographs elsewhere in this chapter) by determining the dog's comfort level. Some dogs are fearful of an empty hand approaching their face. Others are tolerant of collar touching until a hand reaches over the back of the neck. Always start where the dog is comfortable and work from there.

Subsequent Weeks

Typically, each session from the second week forward starts and ends with the relaxation exercises learned in the first class. Then owners put the muzzles on their dogs and do some calm, individual, on-leash walking/attention exercises. When your dog walks by his or her sitting classes, provide lots of positive reinforcement for calm behavior. Next, you'll likely try "pass-bys," where two dogs pass each other walking on leash, again with lots of treats for good behavior.

After the relaxation and leash exercises, the first off-leash interaction is conducted. Owners are told when to release their dogs—and then to simply stand back out of the way. Confrontations between the dogs are likely during this time, but the muzzles prevent injury.

The first off-leash interaction likely will be a high anxiety time for everyone in the class. Usually, you'll be cautioned to let the instructor handle any problems. Often, any confrontations will last just moments. You'll also likely see the dogs wander around the training area, glaring but not attacking. The instructor typically after a few minutes will tell the owners to call their dogs, reward them, put the leashes back on, remove the muzzles, and settle in for relaxation and debriefing.

In subsequent classes, the instructor will ask you to use the off! interrupter to try to head off confrontations (with a big click and reward if the dogs succeeded), and gotcha! to intervene if necessary. You'll be asked to practice these two cues at least twenty minutes per day between class sessions.

While There's Still Time

There is a crying need to help dogs remember how to be part of a pack. Dog-aggressive breeds, poorly socialized pups, and dogs encouraged or allowed to be aggressive with each other are a result of human, not canine, failure. Dogs are designed to live and work together in relative harmony, and we have botched the plan.

But for many dogs, it is not too late. If you have a dog who wants to eat other dogs for breakfast, find your nearest positive reinforcement trainer (who will use treats, praise, and other rewards rather than choke or pinch collars) and ask for assistance. If you're lucky, he or she may start a socialization class soon. ■

Off! Part I

Off! has applications far beyond a socialization class. Off! means "Whatever you are paying attention to, I want you to leave it alone." You must program your dog to understand that what you are going to give him or her is infinitely more desirable than the object you're asking the animal to ignore. Most dogs can learn to ignore treats on the ground directly in front of them in just one short session.

Clockwise, from top left: The dog is offered a treat inside a closed fist and told "Off!"—once only, in an upbeat tone. She licks and paws the hand, trying to get the treat. 2) She keeps trying to get the treat. The trainer waits without repeating "Off!" 3) Confused, the dog pulls back her nose. 4) Immediately, the trainer clicks! or says "Yes!" and offers a treat from the other hand. This exercise is repeated until the dog pulls her nose away from the forbidden treat the instant the trainer says "Off!" and continues to leave it alone when the trainer opens her hand with the treat. If the dog dives for the open hand, the trainer closes her fist, says "Click!" and offers a treat only when the dog pulls away.

Off! Part II

This is the beginning of the practical application of Off! Create a course by setting up several small piles of treats in an open area. Pavement is best—it's too hard to see your treat piles in grass.

The more you practice, the more reliable your dog will become in real-world situations.

One tip: if your dog is having trouble with this, start by using really boring treats on the ground and wonderful ones in your hand, so the reward for doing the off! is infinitely better than grabbing the pile.

Clockwise from top left:
1. The dog sees the treat pile and heads for it. The trainer says "Off!" and gently restrains her so she can't reach it. Then she invites her to come with a tasty treat. As soon as the dog turns away from the pile, she gets a "Yes!" or a click! and the treat.

2. On the second pass, she resonds immediately to the "Off!" cue, and

3. gets a click! and a jackpot—a whole handful of treats for her wonderful behavior.

Off! With Another Dog

In a socialization class, all dogs are relaxed on their rugs while one dog is walked on leash far enough away from others to avoid triggering aggression. When the walking dog glances at another dog, the owner gives the off! cue and rewards the appropriate response.

As the dogs become skilled at this, off! is used during other exercises and interactions. Using off! with non-threatening interactions will increase the reliability of your dog's response when faced with potentially aggressive situations in real life. If he or she notices another dog, five the off! cue and reward your dog when both eyes are back on you.

1. *The dog eyes a strange dog at her house with suspicion. If this were a class, the second dog's owner would be kneeling next to him doing relaxation exercises.*

2. *Next, the first dog makes a little rush straight for the second. Her owner quickly gives the off! cue and invites her away with a treat.*

3. When the dog responds appropriately, she gets the click! and reward. By the third pass, the dog turns away from the other dog on the off! and looks for her reward.

4. By the fifth pass, she doesn't even bother to look at the other dog. Mission accomplished!"

Treating
Noise-Phobic Dogs

*Desensitizing a dog with noise phobias is
possible, but takes it time and patience.
Don't look for a quick and easy fix.*

Many behaviorists and dog trainers believe that puppies go through a so-called "fear imprinting" period sometime between the ages of eight to twenty weeks, when they learn what is safe in the big wide world, and what is not. Exposure to traumatic stimuli—thunderstorms, fireworks or other loud noises—can have long-lasting effects.

The same exposure after this critical period might temporarily frighten a dog, but is much less likely to do permanent damage to a dog's psyche. Obviously then, the first step in dealing with noise phobias is prevention. During this "fear imprinting" period of a young pup's life, it is imperative to take extra precautions to see that he or she isn't traumatized by unusually loud or sudden noises.

Even later on in a dog's life, it is important to avoid experiences, such as confining the dog near a noise-producing object, that might trigger an unhealthy fear of loud noises. And there may actually be a genetic predisposition for the development of fearful behaviors, which would help to explain why one dog can tolerate repeated noisy stimuli with impunity, while another needs only one exposure to the same stimulus to develop a severe behavior problem.

But what do we do about the thousands of noise-phobic dogs for whom prevention is no longer an option? The damage has already been done. Are they doomed to spend the rest of their lives hiding under the bed or trying to dig a hole in the floor whenever storm clouds gather?

It is a serious concern. Animal shelters universally report that July 5 and January 1 are the two busiest days of the year because they're caring for dogs who escaped the night before. Fear-induced adrenaline causes dogs to scale fences that would normally be more than adequate to keep them safely confined. Some even go through plate-glass windows and dig through doors in their frantic attempts to escape the torment of the noise.

Noise-phobic dogs may react to firecrackers, gunshots, cars back-firing, cap guns, wood chopping, falling pots and pans, or any other loud noise. But by far the most common stimulus that triggers noise phobia in dogs is the thunderstorm. Storms offer a number of potential fear-producing stimuli, including the noise of thunder, wind and rain, flashes of lightning, changes in atmospheric pressure, ionization, and storm-related odors.

Treatments

Fortunately, there are ways to desensitize noise-phobic dogs. It takes time and a real commitment on the part of the dog owner to do so, but noise desensitization programs, if followed faithfully, do have a good chance of succeeding.

While all the aforementioned stimuli may play a role in thunderstorm phobia, the most overpowering and easiest of them to replicate for modification work is the noise component.

The two most common approaches to behavior modification involve either desensitization and counterconditioning, or flooding and habituation. Used in conjunction with behavior modification, drugs can be used successfully to address noise phobias.

Desensitization/counterconditioning and flooding/habituation are opposite approaches; you can't do both at the same time. Flooding can be extremely traumatic, and once embarked upon must be followed to its conclusion to be successful. This can take many hours, and if the session is stopped before the dog relaxes and accepts the noise, it is likely to just make the problem worse; the dog may think that it was the fearful behavior that finally succeeded in making the noise stop. Flooding is commonly used in the treatment of human fears and phobias, but much less so in dogs.

Desensitization and counterconditioning, on the other hand, are used together frequently and successfully to overcome canine fears. We can't use real storms in a desensitization program. Real storms happen too quickly to allow for the gradual increase in intensity that is necessary for desensitization to succeed. However, we can create artificial, controllable thunderstorms through the creative use of stereo equipment, recordings of thunder, strobe lights (to simulate lightning), and sprinklers or hoses to create the sound of rain on the window or roof.

Behavioral Definitions

- **Phobia:** *A non-useful, counterproductive fear response that is out of proportion to the real level of threat posed by the stimulus.*

- **Counterconditioning:** *A technique by which an animal is conditioned to respond in ways that are incompatible with an undesirable response by gradually presenting the feared stimulus while the animal is engaged in a pleasurable activity (such as eating food). Ideally, the stimulus is presented at a level that does not evoke a fear reaction at any time. (This method usually is performed simultaneously with desensitization.)*

- **Desensitization:** *A technique used to reduce fear responses in a step-by-step process by exposing the animal initially to non-fearful stimuli and gradually increasing the intensity of the stimuli without evoking a fear response.*

- **Flooding:** *A fear-removal technique whereby an animal is continuously exposed to a full-strength fear-causing stimulus until the animal stops exhibiting the fearful behavior. The stimulus is not removed until some time after the animal has completely relaxed. At the end of the session, the animal is experiencing the full-strength stimulus in a non-fearful state of mind.*

- **Habituation:** *The decrease or loss of response to a fear-inducing stimulus solely as the result of repeated exposure to that stimulus without the use of pleasant or aversive associations (rewards or punishments).*

The Desensitization Program

Begin your behavior modification program by finding a recording (or combination of recording and other stimuli) that causes your dog to react fearfully. Thunderstorm recordings on tape or CD are available at most music outlets. As soon as the dog begins to show fear of the stimuli, turn them off. You don't want to evoke a full fear response; you just want to find the level at which your dog begins to respond.

Once the dog is totally relaxed again, you can begin the training program. Start by playing the recording below the level that would evoke a fearful response. This may be at a level that you cannot even hear. Remember that your dog's hearing is infinitely better than yours. After five minutes or so, increase the sound slightly. (This is the desensitization part.) While your dog is still calm, feed him or her absolutely wonderful treats – roast beef or steak, fried chicken skins, or anything else that your dog would normally do backflips for. (This is the counterconditioning part.) You want your dog to think that wonderful things happen when thunderstorm noises occur.

Be generous with the terrific treats, petting, and praise, and keep the sound at each level for several minutes before gradually increasing the volume again. At some point, your dog will start to exhibit a mild, fearful reaction. (If it is not mild, you have increased the volume too quickly.) Watch for panting, pacing, clinging to you, and other signs of tension.

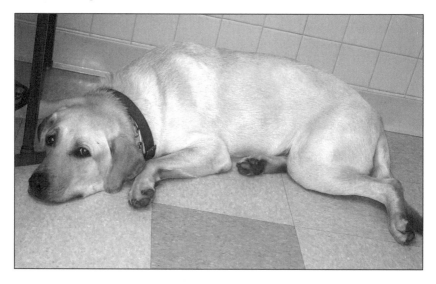

When this happens, you have two choices. You can immediately turn the volume back down or wait and see if the dog habituates to that level of intensity. If the reaction is truly mild and you have been very gradually increasing the volume, it is preferable to wait for habituation.

Keep the volume at this level for a considerable period of time before increasing the volume again; the amount of time depends on the dog. As soon as the dog relaxes—when the signs of stress go away—resume treat-feeding and petting.

Move Forward Slowly

It is important not to play the recording too loudly or to increase the volume too quickly. Increasing the stimulus level too rapidly is the most common mistake made in desensitization programs. It is very important not to evoke a fear response that does not habituate during the session; this would be a major step backward. Be patient. While the first few sessions may proceed slowly, subsequent sessions usually will go much faster. It often takes only three to five sessions to move past the initial volume level at which the dog first reacted fearfully. This can be accomplished in less than a week.

Once your dog accepts loud thunderstorm noises, reduce the volume and add the other stimuli, one at a time, until he or she is comfortable with the entire package. Each time you add a new stimulus, reduce the intensity of the others and gradually increase them again, one at a time.

You will also want to change locations from time to time, so the dog accepts the stimuli package in any room of the house. Later on, the onset of the artificial storm should occur outside of formal training sessions, perhaps first while the dog is playing with a favorite toy or eating dinner, then at random times.

When your dog is comfortable with storm noises in all of these situations, you can set your storm on a timer to play at very low levels for very short intervals (at first) when you are not home. Remember: every time you change an aspect of the exercise, you must reduce the intensity of each element of the package.

For noises other than storms, it is a matter of finding an adequate artificial replication of the offending noise and any other relevant stimuli that can be incorporated into a similar program.

A Shocking Theory

Some people believe that it is the buildup of static electricity (and resultant static shocks to the dog) that occurs during a thunderstorm that makes many dogs develop an extreme fear of storms.

This would explain why some dogs hide in bathtubs or wedge themselves behind toilets when a storm hits. Their contact with the porcelain plumbing fixtures is thought to ground them and protect them from shocks. Many storm-phobic dogs are much calmer if they are allowed to "ride out" the storm in a car—maybe because the car provides some protection from the storm sounds as well as from static shocks.

Some owners report success with laundry no-cling strips. Rubbing these sheets over the dog can also prevent static shocks. It is not an unreasonable theory. The intensity of many dogs' reactions to storms is comparable to the extreme reaction often seen by dogs who are subjected to shocks from electronic training collars. Driving your dog around in a car during a storm or rubbing him or her with anti-static laundry sheets are easy and inexpensive solutions to try.

While not every noise-phobic dog can be successfully desensitized, behaviorists report a fair degree of success with such programs. This is good news to the owners of the thousands of noise-phobic dogs who suffer through thunderstorms and other fear-inducing sounds.

How Long Does It Take?

Studies indicate that frequent desensitization/counter-conditioning sessions of thirty to forty-five minutes are more effective than multiple short ones. Mild to moderate phobias may be successfully treated in just a few weeks. Severe cases can take longer. A month or more is not unusual and, unfortunately, sometimes the dogs never come around. Studies of desensitization programs for extremely noise-phobic dogs are not very encouraging. However, this may be because the dogs weren't being desensitized to the right stimulus. It is important to mimic as many of the elements of the package of thunderstorm stimuli as possible for the greatest chance of success.

It is beneficial to accomplish desensitization as quickly as possible. If a real storm occurs during the training process and traumatizes the dog it can set the training back. Where storms are seasonal, it makes sense to start and complete the program during the "off-season. Because the desensitization can apparently fade with time, it is also a good idea to refresh the training once or twice a month. ■

9

Does Your Dog Bite?

Biting is a natural, normal dog behavior, and every dog has a threshold that shouldn't be crossed.

The trainer had been playing with the 120-pound, confident, intact male Rottweiler for more than forty-five minutes. He sat next to him and leaned happily against his leg. Without thinking, the trainer bent down and reached across the back of the dog's neck to scratch behind his ear.

In a split second, the dog's eyes went cold and the trainer felt, rather than heard, the rumble of a growl from deep within the dog's throat. He whirled away from the Rottweiler's massive jaws just in time to catch the bite in the padded shoulder of his jacket, rather than his face. He stood perfectly still, heart thudding, legs weak, waiting to see what the dog would do next. But the dog sat back down, smiled a big Rottweiler grin and wagged his stump of a tail.

"No hard feelings," he was saying, "as long as you mind your place."

The professional dog trainer should have known better. The dog's sensibilities as a dominant male had been offended by the trainer's audacity to reach over the back of his neck, a serious challenge in dog-speak. Only luck and quick reactions saved the trainer from being badly bitten in the face. A child, a senior citizen, or any unsuspecting person in this situation could easily have ended up at the nearest emergency room, headed for the reconstructive surgery.

Common Problem

Biting is a natural, normal dog behavior, something we tend to forget. All dogs are potential biters. This is why dog bites are so prevalent—statistically, the number one health problem for children in this country, surpassing measles, mumps, and whooping cough combined, according to the National Centers for Disease Control in Atlanta.

The CDC estimates that more than 4.7 million people are bitten by dogs each year, and 800,000 of those bites are serious enough to require medical attention. Children represent about half of that total. Some 386,000 bites require treatment in an emergency room, and about a dozen people die. The rate of dog bite-related injuries is highest for children ages five to nine.

Children are the most common dog bite victims due to their size, vulnerability, and tendency to move quickly and make strange noises, especially when excited or frightened. Almost two-thirds of injuries among children ages four and younger are to the head or neck, and injury rates are significantly higher among boys.

A great deal has been written about how to avoid being bitten, and there are education programs in schools across the country to teach children how to be safe around dogs. While this effort is commendable, it is equally important to address the canine end of the bite equation.

Anyone who has ever owned a dog who has bitten a person knows the stress of living with a known biter, the guilt of seeing stitches in a child's face, and the agony that comes with making the painful decision to have a dog euthanized rather than risk injury to another human.

If we had a better understanding of how our dogs' minds work, we could prevent many bites from happening and successfully rehabilitate many dogs who have become problem biters through mismanagement and inappropriate training.

The Bite Threshold

According to author and dog trainer Jean Donaldson in her book, *Culture Clash*, dogs, like humans, have a breaking point beyond which if pushed they will respond with aggression. She calls this the "bite threshold." Dogs also have thresholds for other threat behaviors such as growling, snarling, and snapping.

Anything that stresses the dog is a risk factor. Risk factors vary from one dog to the next but can include things like loud noises, children, anything the dog associates with punishment (a leather strap, rolled-up newspaper, choke chain), and anything to which the dog has not been adequately socialized, such as strange men, umbrellas, or odd hats.

> 66 DOGS, LIKE HUMANS, HAVE A BREAKING
> POINT BEYOND WHICH, IF PUSHED, THEY
> RESPOND WITH AGGRESSION. 99

The list of possible risk factors is endless. Any one risk factor may be enough of a stimulus to cross a particular dog's bite threshold, but in many cases it is a combination of factors that join together to push a dog past his or her limit.

For example, let's say your dog is not overly fond of small children, he's afraid of loud noises, and a little bit protective of his toys. One day your two-year-old granddaughter is visiting during a thunderstorm, and crawls over to the dog, who is lying in the corner on the floor next to his favorite toy. The dog, who has always in the past just avoided the toddler, is on edge from the thunder, feels cornered and can't get away, and sees the girl reaching out toward his most valuable possession. "Without warning," he lunges and grabs the little girl's face.

In fact, there was plenty of warning, if someone had recognized the dog's nervousness with each of the individual risk factors and

A dog who signals an intent to bite, like the one above, is actually a far safer companion than a dog who has been punished for this behavior and then learned to suppress it. When exposed to enough stress, the latter will inevitably bite, probably without warning.

understood that putting them all together placed the child at a significant risk of being attacked.

Classifications of Aggression

We tend to think of aggression as being one of two types: dominance aggression, where the dog thinks he or she is the pack leader and bites to get his or her way, or submission aggression, also known as fear aggression, where the shy, timid dog bites when he or she feels cornered or threatened.

In reality, the analysis of aggression is much more complex than this. There are more than a dozen identifiable classifications of aggression, each with different triggers and approaches for modifying the aggressive behavior. Most dogs who have a problem with inappropriate aggression display more than one type. A competent trainer or behaviorist will be able to accurately identify and work with all of the various types of aggression that a dog may manifest.

The Positive Approach

There was a time when the generally accepted method of correcting a dog's aggression was to be more aggressive than the dog. If your dog growled at you when you jerked on his or her leash or tried to force the animal to lie down, you were instructed to "pop" him or her under the chin with a closed fist. If the dog snapped at you in response, you might have been told to do a "scruff shake" or "alpha roll." If the animal continued to fight you, your trainer might have taken the leash from you to "hang" or "helicopter" the dog. These techniques are as abusive as they sound. Dogs have been blinded, permanently brain-damaged, and even killed by these methods. Even so, some trainers continue to use and defend the use of hanging and helicoptering even today.

But progressive, humane trainers have come to understand that aggression begets aggression. Many dogs respond to a physical correction by escalating their own aggression in self-defense. Unless you are willing and able to out-escalate the dog, the dog "wins" the fight and the aggression worsens. Even if you succeed in overpowering the dog, all you have done is suppress the signs of aggression; the risk factors for the aggressive behavior are still there. You have simply taught the dog not to growl or snap in warning.

When you suppress the warning signs of aggression—the growl-

ing and snarling—you actually increase the risk of a serious bite, since the aggression is then more likely to erupt into a full-scale attack without giving you the chance to be warned off by the growl.

Desensitize the Dog

A far better approach is to desensitize the dog to risk factors is to change the way he or she thinks about them. The fewer risk factors a particular dog has, the less likely they are to join in a combination powerful enough to push the animal over the threshold and cause him or her to bite. In the scenario given above, if the dog can learn to think that having children around is a good thing, he will no longer be nervous when they are near, and the presence of children can be eliminated as a risk factor.

You might want to start out by discontinuing the practice of punishing the dog when children are around. If he growls at a child and then the dog is hit or his leash is jerked, the belief that bad things happen when children are around has been reinforced. If the dog is excluded from the family when children visit, that's further negative reinforcement. If, instead, you can consistently make good things happen when children are around, the dog will begin to look forward to their presence.

This shift can be accomplished through the use of a reward marker, such as the click! of a clicker, or the word yes! This is easier if you have already taught the dog to associate the word or sound with a tasty treat, as explained earlier in this book. You might begin your desensitization process by finding a location where children are far enough away that your dog can see them but not feel threatened by them . It helps to employ children whom you know and can instruct to stay away for this purpose. When the dog notices the children, click! the clicker and feed him a treat. Each time he glances at the children and remains calm, click! and treat. This will begin to teach him that seeing children (and remaining calm) is a good thing—children mean treats!

Gradually move closer, continuing to click! and to offer treat for calm behavior. Don't push your luck. If you notice the tiniest sign of nervousness on the dog's part as you approach the children, stop and calmly retreat. If children come toward you, attracted by the dog, use a clear, firm, but calm tone and tell them to stay back!

Dominant stare or hard concentration? Without knowing the dog well, it would be unwise to stare back or to push farther forward into the dog's personal space. The safest tack would be to interpret this look as a warning.

When employing a desensitization program, you need to avoid triggering the behavior you are trying to eliminate. Getting the dog too stressed and forcing him to growl or snap at a child would be a serious setback to your program. Watch closely, and stop at the first sign of discomfort. If you have moved forward in small steps you may be able to pause for a moment, wait for calm behavior to return, and click! and treat the dog for making a good choice of behaviors. If you have been impatient and moved forward too quickly, you may have to back up to find the point where the dog's calm behavior returns, and click! and reward him there. It is always better to move forward slowly and end on a positive note than have to back up and repair damage.

Once you are close enough and the dog is still calm, you can ask the children to toss treats to him so that he starts realizing that good things actually come from the children themselves. Be aware that it may take days, weeks, or even longer to get a dog who is very fearful of children to this point. Ask the children not to stare into the dog's eyes, as this is a strong threat for a dog. And be sure to do this exercise, at least at first, with children you trust to be calm and not act fearful themselves. Over time, you should start to see signs—wagging tail, bright eyes, perked ears—that your dog is eagerly anticipating his encounters with kids instead of fearing them.

Prevention Preferred

It is far easier to prevent undesirable behavior than it is to correct it. A desensitization program can take anywhere from several weeks to months or even years, depending on the intensity of the dog's discomfort with the risk factor and the owner's or trainer's skill. And while you may succeed in desensitizing the dog in the above example to the child factor, you haven't even begun to address his protection aggression over his favorite toy.

If you start when your dog is a puppy and you raise him or her correctly, you can avoid a lot of the headache and heartache of risk factors through proper socialization. Socialization means getting used to environmental elements through exposure.

In the wild, a puppy is naturally exposed to the elements of the world during the first several months of puppyhood. Anything new he or she encounters after that is cause for alarm or at least for extreme caution. The same thing is true of our domesticated puppies. If you make an effort to expose pups to lots of different stimuli during the first five months of their lives, they will grow up with a much shorter list of risk factors. Of course, the exposure must be positive; exposure to traumatizing stimuli during this same period will make the list longer! Renowned trainer Ian Dunbar suggests that people hold occasional "puppy parties" for this purpose; the diverse attendees all wear funny hats and act strangely, and they all take turns praising and feeding the puppy treats!

If you want your puppy to get along with other dogs, give him or her plenty of opportunities to play with other puppies and appropriate (non-aggressive) adult dogs at a young age. If you want your dog not to be possessive of food and toys, spend time gently showing him or her that you can take toys and food away and give them back, or that if you approach while he or she is eating you may provide more or better food. Do this without punishment, and your dog will learn to associate pleasant things with each of these stimuli.

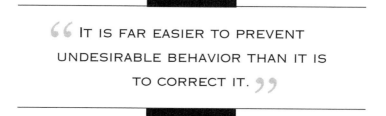

66 IT IS FAR EASIER TO PREVENT UNDESIRABLE BEHAVIOR THAN IT IS TO CORRECT IT. 99

Fearful Puppies

Some puppies are born more fearful than others. It is especially important to take the time to socialize these shy guys, or they can turn into serious fear biters. Because of the gap that can occur between protection from maternal antibodies and puppyhood vaccines, some veterinarians counsel their clients to keep puppies confined at home until at least the age of four months. Unfortunately, while these pups may never die of distemper or parvovirus, they risk losing their homes and perhaps their lives because of the socialization that they miss during their critical learning period. Far more dogs are euthanized due to behavior problems caused by lack of socialization and training than puppies who contracted diseases from exposure to other dogs.

Many training classes now start puppies as young as ten weeks as long as they as they are properly vaccinated in an effort to provide socialization and early training for the youngsters. These pups never have a chance to learn wrong behaviors, since they learn the right ones from a very early age—as long as the trainer uses positive, non-punitive training methods and no choke chains.

Get Help

If you have a dog who already has lots of risk factors, seek help from a competent professional soon rather than later. Don't wait until a tragedy occurs to recognize your dog's potential to bite, and don't fall into the denial trap. If your dog reacts to a lot of risk factors, or reacts strongly to any one particular factor, likelihood is high that sooner or later he will be pushed past his bite threshold.

Remember, all dogs can bite. When you interview trainers, check their credentials, and be relentless in your questioning about their methods.

And what of the Rottweiler who wanted to eat the trainer? He wasn't a client; the trainer was there on his ranch with a humane officer to investigate a complaint of horse neglect, so there was no chance to work with the Rott to modify his behavior. And he is still out there—a time bomb, running loose on the ranch, that sooner or later will explode in the face of someone who doesn't turn away in time. There are far too many such time bombs out there. Don't let your dog be one of them. ■

10

The Timid Dog

Dogs need to be exposed early and often to a variety of "outside world" experiences—for their own safety and for yours.

Dogs aren't born full-fledged man's best friends. As with all baby animals, there is a period of time in their lives when they must learn about the world to survive. This sensitive period is a window of opportunity for socialization—a time when puppies learn what is safe and good and what is not. Opinions differ as to how long the window is open, but it falls somewhere in the period between four and twenty weeks. After the window closes, anything not previously identified as safe has the potential to fall into the unsafe category. Dogs must be socialized to the human world during this time, or they will have the potential to be fearful of—or, at the very least, anxious about—new people, sights, and sounds.

Socialization: Learned, Not Innate

Dogs who are well-socialized receive lots of gentle human contact and handling from the time their eyes open on into adulthood. Guide Dogs for the Blind and other service dog organizations who must produce the calmest, most socialized dogs possible send their puppies to live with 4-H families where the participants try to take their service puppies with them everywhere they go. As they get older (eight to twenty weeks) they are given careful exposure to other stimuli, such as visits to the vet hospital and groomer; walks in town; rides on elevators and escalators; sounds of cars, motorcycles, and skateboards; people of different ages, sexes, and ethnicities; people who dress, talk and move in strange ways; and people with umbrellas, crutches, and wheelchairs.

If you have ever watched a service dog remain calm and responsive to the handler's requests in the midst of a noisy, bustling environment, you have witnessed proof that such a thorough, positive exposure to the outside world really does result in a more confident and well-adjusted dog, one who will easily accept new stimuli, even without prior exposure to that specific experience.

An Ounce of Prevention

Unfortunately, there are many poorly socialized dogs around us. Many are the result of benevolent neglect—dogs who were never taken anywhere, whose owners didn't anticipate the need for them to be socialized.

The easiest way to avoid this problem, as with most serious dog behavior challenges, is through prevention. While your veterinarian, concerned about diseases, may caution you against exposing your new puppy to the real world, failure to do so can result in a poorly socialized adult dog. And, in the long term, lack of socialization can be a bigger threat to your puppy's well-being than the risk of disease.

The answer to this dilemma is to expose a properly vaccinated young dog to a controlled social environment. Take the animal to a well-run puppy class, where the pup can meet lots of different people and lots of healthy puppies. Invite friends of all ages and races over and have them dress up in various "costumes"—odd clothes, hats, umbrellas, sunglasses. Invite children over to play gently and to give the dog treats.

The more positive encounters a dog experiences while the socialization window is open, the more well-adjusted, confident, and gregarious he or she will be as an adult.

A Pound of Cure

If you're the owner of an unsocialized adult dog, don't despair. Steps can be taken to make the world a less terrifying place for these canines. The quality of their lives can be improved with desensitization and with training that gives them confidence and helps them make sense of the world around them. It takes a lot of work and a patient owner, but it can be done.

The methods used to rehabilitate an unsocialized dog must be positive ones. The poor animal is already terrified of the world. Progress is slow in the best of circumstances, and once the dog starts taking tentative steps to emerge from his or her shell, the tiniest correction can send the animal scurrying back to safety. Each dog will progress at his or her own pace. Be patient; pushing an unsocialized dog too quickly can destroy weeks, even months, of painstaking progress.

Encouraging Courage

Teach your dog a bridge, or reward marker. A bridge is a word or a sound that tells your dog that he or she has earned a reward. The clicker, a small plastic box that makes a clicking sound when pressed, is often used as the bridge in dog training. Your unsocialized dog may be sound-sensitive. If so, you may want to start with a one-syllable bridge word, such as "Yes!" instead of the clicker. "Good dog!" is not a good choice for a reward marker. It's too long. A dog can do several behaviors during the time it takes you to say two syllables. Which one is getting rewarded? Besides, we tend to say "Good dog!" to our dogs all the time just because we love them. We need a marker that only means "a reward is coming."

1. To teach the bridge to your dog, just say "Yes!" (or click! the clicker if he or she will tolerate the sound), and immediately provide a small but very tasty treat. The animal doesn't have to do anything special to get the Yes! and treat at first, but do try to avoid marking and treating if he or she is doing something unacceptable such as jumping on you.

If the dog is unsocialized even with you and won't come close enough to eat treats out of your hand, toss the treats from a distance or scatter them all over the ground and use the yes! or click! cues every time one is picked up. Once your dog knows that the marker means "Treat!" you can, for the rest of his or her life, click! (or yes!) and provide a reward for something done right; this will reinforce that behavior and increase the likelihood that he or she will do it again.

2. *Reward-mark the animal's entire meal. Let this be the only way your dog gets to eat—by being in your company and eventually, when he or she is brave enough, by eating out of your hand. The dog needs to learn that you are the source of all good things.*

3. *Reward-mark your dog for calm behavior around others. Once the dog understands that the bridge means a treat, you can yes! or click! and offer a treat anytime bravery is displayed. If he or she is normally afraid of children and sits quietly next to you on a park bench while a child walks by, yes! and reward. Look for very small, rewardable behaviors. If your dog glances at a child and doesn't react, yes! and reward.*

4. *Make a list of your dog's "fear triggers." You probably have a good idea of what frightens this animal. These are "fear triggers." Decide the trigger with which you want to begin the desensitization program. Start with something achievable; for your dog's sake and for yours, it's important to have small successes throughout the process. If one is a particularly big trigger, you might have to figure out how to break it down into smaller pieces.*

For example: If the Number 1 Trigger is tall men with beards and cowboy hats, you might start with tall, clean-shaven men. Start leaving cowboy hats around the house in conspicuous places, and occasionally put one on yourself. Other family members and people who are well-liked by your dog can do the same. Once he or she accepts tall men, you can advance to clean-shaven tall men with cowboy hats. Meanwhile, work at desensitizing the dog to short men with beards. Then try tall men with beards without cowboy hats. When you have desensitized him or her to all the of the pieces, then you can finally put them together as tall men with beards wearing cowboy hats.

This takes time and patience. If you skip steps, or go too fast, you may undo all of your painstaking training progress and have to start over.

5. Use counterconditioning and desensitization.
Desensitization is the process of gradually acclimating
a dog to the things he or she fears. Counterconditioning
means replacing her undesirable reaction—fear—with a
more desirable one that is incompatible with fear, such
as the eager anticipation of a tasty treat.

6. Reward-mark while others feed treats. The ultimate
goal is to have your dog believe that people are safe and
good, not scary and dangerous. The more your dog will
accept treats from others, the more he or she can associ-
ate them with good things, not just you.

7. Teach your dog to target. "Targeting" is teaching your
dog to touch a target with his or her nose on cue. It's easy
to do, and it's a great confidence builder for timid dogs.
*   To start, hold a target object—such as your hand, a*
pencil, or a short (two- to three-foot) dowel—in front of
you. Use something that won't frighten the animal. When
he or she touches the target with the nose, click! or say
yes! and offer a treat. If the dog won't touch the target,
rub a meaty-flavored treat on it so it smells irresistible.)
When he or she is eagerly touching the target, add the
cue word "Touch!" Continue to click! and treat. In short
order, your dog will be eager to touch the target when you
ask him or her to do so.
*   Dogs love this exercise. It's like a treat vending*
machine—push the button, get a treat. By placing the
target, which they love, near something about which
they are leery, you can get them to approach the scary
object. When they get clicked and treated for touching
the target near the object, they soon decide that the scary
thing isn't so bad.

Don't Overprotect!

Tempting as it may be, do not allow yourself to coddle and comfort
your fearful dog. This rewards and reinforces the timid behavior
rather than building up the animal's confidence. If you act concerned, your dog will be even more convinced that there is something of which to be afraid. Instead, act matter of fact, jolly him or
her up, and let the dog know there's nothing wrong. The target stick

works really well in place of coddling.

Remember, your unsocialized dog is not acting out of spite or malice. This animal is truly afraid, even terrified, of the things to which he or she reacts. Help your dog to learn—slowly—that the world is not such a frightening place after all. ■

11

Feeling Jumpy

*Keeping four on the floor
is simply a matter of basic training
and positive reinforcement.*

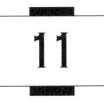

ity the poor canines when it comes to figuring out what humans want. They greet each other by sniffing noses, but when they try to give us a polite canine greeting by jumping up to sniff our faces, we yell, knee them in the chest, smack them on the nose, grab their front paws, squirt lemon juice in their mouths, or stomp on their hind feet.

And these are just some of the punitive methods that have been applied in an effort to teach dogs not to jump on humans. **The most effective solution is simple and nonviolent**: Reward the behavior that you want to reinforce, and ignore the behavior that you want to discourage.

Dogs often are rewarded for jumping. When puppies are small, we pick them up and cuddle them, teaching them that "up" is a very nice place to be. When dogs jump, someone usually pets them or pays attention to them, rewarding the very behavior that should be discouraged. Dogs who find they get rewarded for jumping will just keep doing it.

For some dogs, even the coercive techniques that are meant to be punishments are perceived as rewards—plenty of Labrador Retrievers consider a knee in the chest an invitation to a vigorous game. But how do we ignore jumping? When we simply stand still, a jumper can get our attention by slapping his or her paws on our chest.

The most effective exercises and management tools show your dog that keeping all four paws on the ground can be much more rewarding than any aerial maneuvers.

Consistency is important. Never reward jumping up, and be sure to ask your friends and family members to react appropriately to the dog's antics, too. Behaviors that are rewarded randomly can become very strong—the dog learns that if he or she just keeps trying, sooner or later, jumping will be rewarded. Yes, your dog occasionally will still succeed in jumping on you, but don't encourage this behavior with hugs or petting when it happens.

If you begin these training exercises with a young puppy, you will never have to deal with an adult dog who leaps and jumps. Adult dogs can be retrained, but it's much simpler if the dog never learns the behavior in the first place!

Training Exercises

#1: The On-leash Jump With Strangers

Hold your dog on a leash next to you. Ask a helper to approach the dog and stop just out of leash range, holding a treat against her chest. Hold the leash and stand still. Now, wait. The animal will be frustrated that he or she can't jump on the helper and will sit down to ponder this dilemma. As soon as that happens, ask the helper to say "Yes!" and pop the treat in the dog's mouth. Relax the tension on the leash so the dog is holding the sit on his or her own and is not being restrained.

After about six repetitions, your dog will start to sit as the helper approaches. If he or she tries to leap up to get the treat when it's offered, have the helper whisk it out of reach and say in a cheerful voice, "Too bad!" When the dog sits again, the helper should say "Yes!" and offer the treat. Your dog will soon learn that the treat comes by sitting tight, not by jumping.

If you prefer, you can say "Yes!" and pop the treat in the dog's mouth. This way, he or she will learn to look at you and sit as people approach, instead of looking at the people. Repeat this exercise with as many different helpers as possible. Your dog will learn quickly to sit instead of jump when strangers approach.

#2: The On-leash Jump With You

You may not always have a helper handy, so here's a training exercise you can practice on your own. Attach the leash to a solid object. If your dog chews on the leash, use a tie-down (a plastic-coated cable with snaps at both ends).

Walk about thirty feet away, then turn around and start walking back to your dog. As long as he or she remains seated, keep approaching. The instant there's jumping up, stop walking. When the dog sits, move forward again.

In this exercise, the dog's reward for sitting is simply that you come closer. Provide a food treat if your dog is still sitting when you reach him or her. The treat doesn't have to come every time there's a sit. Try turning your back on the dog or backing up a step when he or she stands, which may encourage a sit even sooner.

“ IF YOU BEGIN THESE TRAINING EXERCISES WITH A PUPPY, YOU WILL NEVER HAVE TO DEAL WITH AN ADULT DOG WHO IS LEAPING AND JUMPING. ”

#3: The Off-leash Jump

You come home and your dog flies over the sofa to greet you. You know exactly what's coming. There's no leash to restrain him or her. What should you do?

This is simple: *turn away*. Watch the dog out of the corner of your eye, and turn and step away as he or she tries to jump. If you consistently repeat this behavior, the animal will eventually sit in frustration. The instant your dog sits, say "Yes!" in a bright voice and offer a treat and petting. If the dog starts to jump again after eating the treat, turn and step away. Repeat this response until your dog realizes that sitting—not jumping—results in the attention he or she craves.

For this exercise, it makes sense to carry treats in your pocket or to keep a jar near the door through which you'll be entering (high enough that the dog can't get to it, of course).

To avoid reinforcing the wrong behavior, be sure to give the yes! marker only when the dog is sitting, not before. Yes! means "Whatever behavior you are doing at the instant that you hear this word has earned you a treat."

Sometimes, a series of behaviors can become connected or "chained" together because the dog thinks the reward follows the performance of all the behaviors, not just the last one.

For example, your dog might learn the short behavior chain of "jump up, sit, get reward." To avoid confusion, frequently reward the dog whenever he or she sits without jumping. The dog quickly will learn exactly which behavior earns the reward.

Time Out

When your jumpy canine is out of control and leaping all over you or your visitors, deliver a cheerful, "Too bad, time out!" and have him spend a few minutes on his or her tie-down.

A tie-down is a plastic-coated cable, about four to six feet long with snaps on both ends. You can secure one end to a heavy piece of furniture or attach it to an eye bolt. Place a comfortable rug or bed nearby.

If you know in advance that your dog is going to leap on a visitor the instant the company arrives, clip him or her to the tie-down before you open the door.

Release your dog when he or she settles down. If, after the release, the dog revs up again, repeat the message: "Too bad, time out!"

Remember, despite your frustration, your tone should be cheerful, not punishing or forceful. The dog will gradually learn to control his or her own behavior to avoid time-outs, and you won't need to scold to keep the animal on all fours.

#4: Alternative Behavior Requests

When your dog approaches, ask for a sit or a down before there's time for jumping. Reward the behavior with a yes! and a treat. After several repetitions, the dog may offer those behaviors before you even ask.

This exercise only works if your dog responds well to the sit and down verbal cues. If that's not the case, and you have to repeat the cues several times—with the animal jumping up on you all the while—you are actually rewarding the dog (with your attention) for bad behavior. The dog is also learning to ignore your verbal cues for sitting and lying down.

#5: Jumping on Cue

This exercise is only recommended if you find a dog's antics endearing and want to encourage him or her to jump *occasionally*. If so, teach the dog a verbal cue for jumping—and that the only time it's okay to jump is when someone gives that cue.

Reward the dog for jumping only after he or she has been invited to jump. Don't pat your chest or include any other gesture when giving the cue, because strangers and children may unknowingly repeat the gesture and signal the dog to jump.

Jumping is a normal, natural behavior for dogs. It is the owner's responsibility to communicate that jumping up—like so many other normal dog behaviors—is unacceptable in human society. Help make your dog a more welcome member of that society by training and rewarding acceptable replacement behaviors. If you start early, it's easier than you think! ■

12

Hark! A Bark!

*How to teach any dog when and how
to bark, and when and how to stop,
using reward-based training methods.*

When does a dog become a "problem barker"? When the neighbors complain? When the noise makes you want to climb the walls? With the exception of some specific breeds, nearly all dogs bark at some time or another. It's a form of communication, after all.

First, ascertain that your dog's barking is not related to a medical condition of some sort—that is, that the animal isn't in pain with a toothache or an injury. A visit with your veterinarian and your own physical examination, gently petting the animal and noting any touch that results in a start or a flinch from your pet, can help identify a physical problem.

Once you've ruled out a medical condition, it's time to determine what your dog is trying to tell you so that you can address his or her concerns and teach other, more acceptable means of communication.

Veterinarian, animal behaviorist and author Ian Dunbar says three methods can be used to alleviate problem barking and to help your dog learn to bark on command when appropriate. The methods are simple management, reward training, and lure/reward training. They may be used together or separately. And, Sabra Learned, a Berkeley, California, practitioner and instructor of Tellington TTouch, shares her thoughts on helping the problem barker.

Simple Management

Whether or not your dog is a problem barker, Dr. Dunbar recommends that the animal be fed only out of chew toys. "Stuff the dog's usual meal into six different chew toys and when you leave in the morning, put them in different locations all over the house. Better yet, tie several different chew toys full of food in the dog's crate with the door open or fasten them to an eye hook in the baseboard next to the dog's bed," Dr. Dunbar says. "To get his dinner, the dog has to go to his resting place and play with his chew toy."

Why do this rather than simply providing meals in a dog bowl? "It's a simple fact that a dog cannot sniff and chew and bark at the same time," he says. "You reduce his opportunities to bark by giving him something constructive to do for a good part of his day. This is especially effective because each piece of kibble rewards the dog for not barking."

Within just a week, Dr. Dunbar says, the dog will not only be barking less, but he or she also will be calmer, will have learned to settle down and enjoy quiet moments, and will have little inclination to become a destructive chewer.

Reward Training

Whether they realize it or not, most owners train their dogs to bark by ignoring the animals when they are quiet and responding to barking. Even if that response is negative—yelling at the dog to be quiet, for example—the owner is paying attention to the animal, which was the goal. "The dog thinks, 'Gosh, this barking thing works great! I just got him to wake up!'" Dr. Dunbar says.

But if your dog gets attention only when he or she has stopped barking and is quiet, the amount of barking will be reduced substantially. Dr. Dunbar does recommend setting a system for rewarding reward appropriate barking. "When the raccoons are breaking into the cat's food on the back porch, or a stranger is standing on your front porch, you want the dog to bark. But a few barks will do it; it doesn't require five hundred barks," he says.

You may want your dog to bark when someone comes to your front door, but then to quiet down quickly while you determine who your visitor is. To work on this behavior, enlist the help of a friend. Ask him or her to ring the doorbell every couple of minutes.

When the bell rings the first time, if your dog begins barking, go to

Murphy's Law of learning: If you put a behavior problem on cue, it becomes an obedient response, says Dr. Dunbar.

the animal and praise it, then wait for the barking to stop. Depending on how serious the barking problem is, this could take as long as twenty minutes. Eventually, the dog will stop. (If you think twenty minutes is likely, advise your friend to bring along a book or magazine.

When the dog has been quiet for at least three seconds, praise him or her profusely, and offer the animal part of the usual dinner rations. Dr. Dunbar recommends this rather than treats, as a good deal of food may be required. After a couple of more minutes, if the dog hasn't resumed barking, offer more kibble.

When your friend has heard nothing but silence for a few minutes, it's time to ring the bell again. Let's assume your dog begins barking again. At this point, Dr. Dunbar advises, say "There's a good dog" gratefully and politely, but not enthusiastically. Wait until the dog stops barking to become enthusiastic—and offer more kibble.

Building on Success

After several repetitions of this routine, you can prompt the dog to start slowing down the barking while he or she still is in the middle of it. Dr. Dunbar suggests using the same pattern as above. "The dog will have learned that he has to be quiet to get the kibble," he says. "Wait for at least three seconds of silence before you give him the treat. If he starts to bark again, ask him again [if he wants a treat], and hold the treat where he can see it." If you can count to three before there's another bark, give the treat.

"The dog is learning two things," Dr. Dunbar says. "The first is, 'Barking is OK, my owner actually kind of likes it, especially when the doorbell rings, but he likes it better when I'm quiet.' Second, he's learning that it's a really great thing to stop barking when you say" to do so.

The veterinarian advises keeping a jar of kibble at the front door to be prepared for those doorbell rings.

"I like reward training; it's very calming," Dr. Dunbar says. "This is because you don't give any commands; you just wait ... the desired behavior will eventually come."

Lure/Reward Training

Owners who have a really good connection with their dogs and who like training can use the lure/reward method to train their dogs when and when not to bark, Dr. Dunbar says. However, he notes that owners must understand that barking is normal dog behavior, and it would be inhumane to stop a dog from barking completely.

"To train the dog to bark on command, we use the old Request—Response—Reward sequence," he says. "We say, 'Speak!'; the dog goes, 'Woof woof'; we say, 'Good dog!' and give him some kibble. Only now, to speed up the training, we are going to lure the dog to bark in a 'Request—Lure—Response—Reward' sequence, with you indoors with your dog and your friend back with his book on the front porch."

This is how it works: you say, with some urgency, "Speak!" Your friend then rings the doorbell, which serves as a lure. Your dog gives the response—a bark. You then praise the dog and reward him or her, and after five to seven seconds of barking, say "Good dog, now shush" and hold kibble in front of the animal. To sniff the kibble, the dog will have to stop barking; praise that behavior, and when the sniffing has lasted two or three seconds, reward the dog with the kibble.

"Repeat this half a dozen times and, if dogs thought like we do, they would muse, 'Hmmm. How do these owners always know when the doorbell is going to ring?'" Dr. Dunbar says. "But what dogs actually figure out is that you always says, 'Speak!' just before the doorbell rings. 'Heck, I'm just going to bark when he says, "Speak!" I'm not going to wait for the doorbell!' The dog has learned that the request always precedes the lure which causes the response, at which point the lure is no longer necessary."

---

66 ...A DOG CANNOT SNIFF AND CHEW
AND BARK AT THE SAME TIME. 99

Advanced Training

Once your dog has mastered the previous lessons, you can differentiate among the various stimuli and which you would and would not like to elicit barking.

"I had a dog once who wanted to bark at every person walking down the sidewalk in front of my house—not an acceptable activity in a quiet neighborhood," Dr. Dunbar says. "However, I do want my dogs to let me know when a person walks into my yard or is coming to my door. So I planned a party one morning, and I deliberately told all of my guests to arrive at different times. I also instructed them to walk up and down the sidewalk six or seven times before walking up the path that leads to my front door. Then I sat with my dog by a window that overlooked the sidewalk and path.

"The dog barked at the first person who walked by, and I said, 'Shush, Shush, Shush,' and did my best to quiet her by holding kibble where she could see it. By the time my friend walked down the sidewalk four times, the dog had become more interested in her kibble, which she sniffed and received as a Shush reward. The next three walk-bys were quiet, and I rewarded my dog with much praise and more bits of kibble.

"Then my friend entered my front path. As his foot struck the first step on the path, I exploded, saying, 'Speak! Speak! Speak!' as if there was some kind of amazing emergency. Startled, the dog let forth a barrage of barking, and I praised her as my friend walked up the path and came in."

Dr. Dunbar notes that his example shows it's possible to modify problem behavior into a positive: "I created the best burglar alarm that money can buy, and best yet, I can sleep with it!"

Why Do They Bark?

Like Dr. Dunbar, Sabra Learned notes that dogs bark to communicate, and that there are times we want our dogs to bark—to notify us of smoke coming from the oven or that there's a prowler outside, for example. "Tellington TTouch recognizes that problem barkers also have a valid message," Learned says. "By paying attention to it, we have the opportunity to engage in a dialogue with our dogs and work cooperatively to establish quieter and more mutually rewarding ways to communicate."

A problem barker's message may be emotional, physical or mental. "Few of us agree that these kinds of messages should be conveyed through an endless volley of barking," she says. "But by acknowledging that the message exists, we can change our perception of it from 'He's doing it on purpose to drive me crazy!' to 'How can I help him express himself more constructively and quietly?'"

Detective Work

The first step in addressing problem barking is to observe the dog in his or her environment and determine the triggers that are setting off the barking. Sometimes, the solutions are easy: "If the dog barks at people going by, put up curtains or close the blinds so the dog can't look out that window," Learned says. If the tone of your doorbell sets your dog off, use a knocker. The more you define, support, and acknowledge their role in the house, the less they'll feel a need to create their own."

Step two using the TTouch technique is to help the barker regain his or her physical, emotional, and mental balance and to teach better, more effective strategies for coping. TTouch works directly on the nervous system, using specific circles, body movements, and learning exercises in a non-habitual way to stimulate body awareness and activate new neural pathways to the brain. Sounds good, but what does it mean?

"Any kind or amount of TTouch will help a compulsive barker, but some of the exercises—what we call the 'mouth work'—are especially appropriate. Barking is an oral occupation, and so by working with the mouth, you help bring the dog's attention to it. For example, a TTeam practitioner might slide their hands across the dog's muzzle, massage and gently stretch the lips, and tap on the tongue and the roof of the mouth," Learned says.

"Another huge benefit of TTouch is it can be learned relatively easily," she says. "The deeper connection it brings between you and your dog—the increase in trust and respect you will receive from listening to and honoring their message—is a priceless gift and a beginning well worth pursuing." ■

13

How Professionals Can Help

*If you're running into training challenges
that seem too deep-rooted for you to
handle on your own, consider seeking
assistance from an expert.*

Sometimes, an owner's love isn't enough to help overcome a
dog's problems. It be that the dog experienced severe trau-
ma early in life, or that others used inappropriate, harmful
techniques to try to deal with those problems. Fortunately,
there are professionals trained to help people whose pets are having behavior problems: certified applied animal behaviorists and
board-certified veterinary behaviorists. Before you can decide what
a particular specialist can do for you, you need to understand what
the individual's qualifications mean.

Certified Applied Animal Behaviorists

The Animal Behavior Society (ABS) is the leading professional organization in North America for the study of animal behavior, and
was the first organization in the United States to offer a certification program for applied animal behaviorists. Certification consti-
tutes recognition by the Animal Behavior Society that the
professional applied animal behaviorist meets the educational, experiential, and ethical standards required by the society.

Certified applied animal behaviorists come from a variety of
backgrounds. However, they all share a common understanding of
animal behavior theory as well as application. Animal behavior-

ists can be educated in several disciplines, including psychology, biology, zoology, and animal science. A professional applied animal behaviorist has expertise in the principles of animal behavior, in the research methods of animal behavior, in applying animal behavior principles to companion animal behavior problems, and in disseminating knowledge about animal behavior through teaching and research.

Educational and experiential requirements are extensive and include a doctoral degree (or masters degree for an associate applied animal behaviorist) from an accredited college or university in a biological or behavioral science with an emphasis on animal behavior and a minimum of five years of professional experience. Another option is a doctorate from an accredited college or university in veterinary medicine plus two years in a university-approved residency in animal behavior and three additional years of professional experience in applied animal behavior.

At this time, there are only thirty-two certified applied animal behaviorists in the United States.

The Tufts Behavior Clinic

Both certified applied animal behaviorists and board-certified veterinary behaviorists are available for consultation through the Tufts Behavior Clinic. Whether you make an in-house clinic appointment or use the PETFAX remote consultation service, you will be asked to complete an extensive questionnaire regarding various aspects of your pet's behavior, health, and lifestyle. Your answers help categorize your pet's unwanted behavior, such as canine aggression.

In the next stage, we make a diagnosis that includes some reference to the reason for the behavior. If you are having problems with aggression, for example, we'll help determine if the dog is challenging family members because of dominance issues or if your interactions are triggering a defensive reaction.

Once we have made an accurate diagnosis, we move into the next stage, a full explanation for the behavior. Understanding what your dog is doing and why often is a big relief and a crucial step in resolving the problem.

This knowledge also helps you develop the patience and understanding necessary to implement the recommended behavior modification strategies.

It is important to understand that many unwanted behaviors are actually normal behaviors that are being performed out of context or inappropriately from your perspective. A dog who is biting strangers is not necessarily a "bad" dog but rather is probably reacting out of fear. Recognizing that the dog is frightened and has no option but to bite a stranger who forces contact should relieve some of your fears and frustrations. That understanding also will help you protect your dog from well-meaning strangers while you learn appropriate behavior modification strategies to help train your dog to become more relaxed.

Once you understand the reason for your dog's behavior, we will develop a behavioral management and treatment program specifically for you and your dog. We offer follow-up via telephone or e-mail to provide support and answer questions as you begin to implement the recommendations. Treatment is holistic in that it embraces all aspects of the pet's life and lifestyle.

Subjects that we address include:
- *The opportunity for exercise and acceptable outlets for innate behaviors,*

- *Communication and training,*

- *Environmental enrichment,*

- *Diet, and*

- *Specific behavior modification programs including "Nothing in Life Is Free" and desensitization and counterconditioning exercises.*

Both the certified applied animal behaviorist and the veterinary behaviorist at Tufts can supply all of the above information. If medical treatment is necessary or psychopharmacologic treatment is indicated, the veterinary behaviorist is qualified to supply this aspect of treatment. The veterinary behaviorist often will perform a physical examination of your dog and order relevant laboratory tests to support the behavioral diagnosis.

For more on the Tufts Behavior Clinic, please see **www.tufts.edu/vet**.

Veterinary Behaviorists

Veterinary behaviorists are veterinarians with a special interest in animal behavior. Some veterinary behaviorists have completed residency programs after graduating from veterinary school and some have passed an exam given by the American College of Veterinary Behaviorists (ACVB).

Diplomates of the ACVB have attained specialist status in veterinary behavior. They are doctors of veterinary medicine who received additional training in clinical veterinary behavior and satisfied the certification requirements of the ACVB. These veterinary behaviorists are board-certified diplomates of the ACVB.

Veterinary behaviorists are trained and licensed to diagnose and treat problems in animals, whether those problems are medical or behavioral. These behaviorists can diagnose medical problems that may be contributing to the animals' behavioral problems. A veterinary behaviorist also is licensed to prescribe drugs and is familiar with psychotropic medications (tranquilizers and antidepressants) and their uses and side effects.

For the Good of the Dog

While applied animal behaviorists cannot treat medical conditions or prescribe medication, many recognize when medical problems are involved or when psychopharmacologic intervention is necessary to resolve the problem. Applied animal behaviorists often will work with your veterinarian to determine the possible medical causes of the behavior problem and can supply drug therapy information that your veterinarian can pursue if he or she feels that pharmacological intervention is necessary to resolve the problem.

Not everyone requires a veterinary behaviorist to help resolve a pet's problems. Certified applied animal behaviorists are well suited to handle non-medical behavior issues. Their scientific background in animal behavior and psychology makes them ideal resources for treating complicated behavioral problems. The human medical equipment of a certified applied animal behaviorist is the psychologist.

Veterinary behaviorists also have some background in animal behavior and learning theory and are qualified to counsel on psychological problems. They are also valuable for diagnosing medical problems that may be associated with behavioral problems and other unwanted behaviors that require psychopharmacologic treatment. Veterinary behaviorists function as animal psychiatrists.

For a directory of certified applied animal behaviorists, visit **www.animalbehavior.org/Applied/CAAB_directory.html**. For a directory of American College of Veterinary Behaviorists diplomates, contact Dr. Steve Feldman at avsabe@yahoo.com. ■

About the Certification Council for Pet Dog Trainers

Editor's Note: This information from the CCPDT Web site is used with permission.

Until the creation of the Certification Council for Pet Dog Trainers in 2001, there was no nationally available certification process for dog trainers.

The CCPDT administered its first test on September 28, 2001, during the Association of Pet Dog Trainers (APDT) annual educational conference. Since then, the test has been administered twice a year at fifteen sites throughout the United States. All test sites are professionally secured and moderated.

This professional testing program was originally created by the Association of Pet Dog Trainers, the largest association of dog trainers in the world. Early on, the APDT recognized the need for certification for its profession. Pet dog trainers needed a credible means of measuring their knowledge and skills and the dog-owning public needed a credible barometer for choosing a trainer.

A task force of approximately twenty nationally known dog training professionals and behaviorists worked for three years to research created the Certification Council for Pet Dog Trainers as a separate, independent council to manage the accreditation and pursue future development.

A candidate who passes the exam earn the title certified pet dog trainer and may use the designation CPDT after his or her name. Certified trainers must earn continuing education credits to maintain their designations.

For more information, contact:
Certification Council for Pet Dog Trainers
Professional Testing Corporation
1350 Broadway, 17th Floor
New York, NY 10018
Phone: (212) 356-0682
Web site: **www.ccpdt.org**

Section III

Training Tools

14

Proper Crate Training

Used appropriately, crates can be valuable training tools and offer your dog a quiet refuge.

In the wild, most canines rely on snug, enclosed areas or dens to bear and raise pups. The den contributes to pack survival and offers protection. It seems that the wild *canis'* yen for denning "persists in domesticated dogs, and den-like settings have a calming effect," says Fred Harrington, a wolf behavior expert and professor of psychology at Mount Saint Vincent University in Halifax, Nova Scotia.

In your home, a warm, snug crate can serve much the same purpose. It works as a housetraining aid (dogs typically won't soil their personal space), a temporary playpen when you can't directly supervise the pup, and a cozy bedroom that can comfort the pup during those first few stressful nights away from littermates.

Crates are, hands down, the safest way for dogs to travel in cars; they are "musts" for canine air travel; and they are a home away from home in hotels where pets are allowed. They offer quiet refuge when a dog is recuperating from an illness or injury and can be a sanctuary when things get hectic around the house. "Every dog should have a place to call its own," notes Dr. Nicholas Dodman, director of the Behavior Clinic at Tufts University School of Veterinary Medicine.

As long as they're not used for punishment, crates can also help correct undesirable canine behaviors such as destructive chewing. More important, crates can help prevent behavior problems before they start by helping owners establish routines for their dogs.

They can be used to help dogs learn two very important skills: eliminating only when and where it is appropriate, and keeping out of trouble.

Why a Crate?

The first proper use of a crate is to teach a dog to eliminate only when and where it is appropriate.

You can teach this to an adult dog within three days. using the "umbilical cord" method: the dog is tied to your waist so you can watch it every second.

Then, every hour on the hour, take the dog outside to the place where he or she can eliminate. Allow at least two minutes. When that happens, give the dog treats, bring him or her back inside, and allow a hour or so of supervised off-leash time. If the dog does not eliminate, don't provide a treat and don't let the animal off-leash. With adult dogs, by the fourth day there usually are no more mistakes.

Puppies may take a little longer to house-train. Your consistency will make all the difference. When at home, confine the puppy whenever you cannot watch him or her every minute. Few dogs or puppies will soil their crates unless they are really desperate; don't keep them in but don't keep the animal in the crate long enough at any one time to become that desperate.

The crate is also a good tool for training the dog about appropriate ways to behave in your home. For example, if the dog's chew toys are kept in the crate, he or she will learn that those toys are good things when the urge to chew and gnaw arises. A side benefit: recreational chewers almost never become annoying chronic barkers.

The dog who finds the crate a pleasurable experience will train him or herself to settle down and enjoy time spent at home alone. After a week or two of this procedure, the adult dog can safely enjoy the full run of the home. (It's not advised that puppies be left alone for any length of time until they are at least twelve months old.)

What Crates Are NOT For

Crates are perhaps second only to choke collars as the most misused dog training equipment. They are not for punishing your dog for doing something wrong; if used in this way, the dog will quickly learn to avoid ever going into the crate, or to be as obnoxious as possible inside the crate to prompt release.

Crates also are not for long-term confinement of puppies *or* adult dogs. Puppies are just like babies; they need to be watched every minute, and few puppy owners seem to understand this. People make arrangements for their new babies to be supervised when they are away from home; they have to learn to do the same with puppies.

When the puppy gets older, say, six to twelve months old, you can begin leaving him or her for longer periods of time. However, you can't just go out the door and hope for the best. You have to teach your puppy how to cope with short-term confinement and, later, with long-term confinement.

For your new adult dog, the most suitable place for teaching long-term confinement would be a bathroom, one with all the toilet paper, towels, shower curtains, and carpets removed. Leave only a few things in there: the dog's bed, an adequate supply of

If you do your job properly, your dog will regard the crate as his or her favorite place to lie down and relax or sleep.

water, some safe hollow chew toys stuffed with food treats, and the dog's toilet. For the latter, something like two short rolls of turf on a sheet of plastic would do. The benefit of this, rather than those commercial puppy pads, is that the dog will train itself to urinate on turf or dirt.

If your new dog is extremely anxious, and takes desperate measures to escape, such as tearing the bathroom door apart, you can't use this method. You will need to consult a professional for advice on dealing with extreme separation anxiety.

The long-term confinement method is a temporary measure, only meant to keep your new dog out of trouble until you have the time for house-training.

> 66 A PUPPY SHOULD REGARD THE CRATE
> AS A PLAYROOM, A DEN, ON A PAR WITH
> CONFINING YOUR CHILD TO A ROOM
> WITH A TV AND VCR, A COMPUTER,
> AND A TON OF TOYS. 99

Crate-training Mistakes

The most common mistake people make with crates is using them as prisons to punish dogs for bad behavior. That's the very best way to teach your dog to avoid going into the crate at any time.

Instead, a dog should regard the crate as a playroom, a den. Confining a dog or puppy to a crate should be on par with confining your child to a room with a TV and VCR, a computer, and a ton of toys.

This is a simple thing to teach puppies. When a puppy is tired and hungry, you put him or her in the crate along with food and some toys. The puppy will eat and then fall asleep.

If someone has taught an adult dog to have apprehensions about the crate, it will probably take at time to allay those feelings. The process will be a little different; the dog will need additional time to get over the anxiety of feeling trapped in the crate. Make the crate an inviting place and slowly lengthen the amount of time you want him or her to spend inside.

Training Theory

The point of training is to make the dog want to do what *you* want him or her to do. How can you make a dog want to be in the crate? Food!

First, always feed your dog inside the crate, and make the most of his or her daily ration by feeding in numerous courses. Put a little food in the crate, let the dog go in and eat it, and then let him or her out right after he's finished. Make the final course of the day a big one, mixing kibble with some juicy canned food. Put the bowl in the crate and then shut the door, with the dog on the outside, and let the dog think about this for a while. After a minute, he or she will be saying, "Hey! Open the crate door! Let me in!" This is what training is all about—let the dog in at this point.

> 66 THE POINT OF TRAINING
>
> IS TO MAKE THE DOG WANT TO DO WHAT
>
> *YOU* WANT IT TO DO. 99

Here's another tactic: Throw a bit of kibble in the crate. Let the dog go in and get it; he or she will come right out again. Do this three or four times. Then, throw a bit of kibble in, and when the dog goes in to get it, shut the door and immediately feed him or her another couple of bits of kibble through the bars. Then, let the dog out, and ignore him or her for three minutes. Next, put a bit of kibble in the crate, shut the door, feed five bits of kibble through the bars, and then let the dog out again and ignore him or her for five minutes.

The next time, put a bunch of kibble in a Kong toy, along with some freeze-dried liver and a bit of honey so it is difficult to get the food out, and put the Kong in the crate. Let the dog in and shut the door. After about ten minutes—before the animal has finished trying to get all the food—open the door, let the dog out, take the Kong away, and ignore him or her for five minutes.

What is the dog learning? That when he or she is in the crate, you provide a lot of attention and food, and there are toys to play with. That crate is okay!

Every dog develops favorite places to lie down. If you've crate-trained your dog properly, that favorite place will be in the crate with the door open. If the dog goes there of his or her own accord, it's a good sign that you have done a good job as a trainer.

Crate-training Tips

- **Open-Door Policy:** *Leave the crate door open until your dog willingly enters and exits on its own. "Dens don't have doors," notes Dr. Dodman.*

- **Activity Alley:** *Hide food treats in a T-shirt with your smell on it in the crate. The dog will associate the crate with stimulating hide-and-seek activities and the security of your "alpha dog" scent.*

- **Doggie Diner:** *Feed your dog in the crate to link the "den" with the ultimate canine joy—eating..*

- **Snooze City:** *Encourage your dog to nap in the crate, another canine joy.*

- **Play Place:** *Praise, play with, and pet your dog when he or she is inside the crate..*

- **Snuggle Space:** *Equip the crate with a warm, soft pad or blanket.*

Crate Criteria

Most crates are made of thick-gauge metal wire or molded plastic. Dr. Dodman prefers the plastic crates because the solid walls provide more privacy and security than the "transparent" wire crates. (You can "wall in" a wire crate by throwing a blanket over the sides and back of it.) Whichever material you choose, your dog's crate should be ruggedly constructed and fitted with secure door latches. For portability, look for crates that disassemble or fold up easily.

Above all, make sure your dog's crate is the appropriate size—at least large enough for your dog to stand up, turn around, and lie down in. But a crate shouldn't be too big—especially for a pup. "Young dogs often find spacious quarters more disturbing than comforting," notes Dr. Dodman. Also, a crate that's too large can sabotage house-training because the pup can eliminate at one end and then move to the other. If you're raising a pup, purchase a crate that will be big enough to accommodate the animal when he or she is grown, then insert partitions or cardboard boxes inside the crate to reduce the interior space for the time being. ■

15

Collars, Harnesses, & Leads

*The tools you use have a big and lasting
effect on training efforts.*

There's a great temptation—especially if you live in the country, although city dwellers are guilty of this as well—to let your pet go about without a collar. Don't! Your dog's collar and leash are important tools for training and restraining. Some owners believe even simple buckle collars can get snagged and choke a dog to death. Although possible, it's highly un-
likely. The potential problems
and dangers collarless dogs face
are far greater. Chief among them:
if your dog has no identification,
it could be a painful—even dead-
ly—experience for him or her.

It's best to get your dog accus-
tomed to wearing a collar as soon
as possible. Whether you're dealing with a puppy or an adult,
your dog probably will resist the
idea at first. To help gain acceptance, let the dog sniff at the collar—but don't let him or her chew
it. If you have a pup, an inexpensive lightweight buckle collar will do the trick, as your pet

will soon outgrow this collar. A five- or ten-dollar nylon fabric or leather buckle collar will do just fine.

The collar should fit comfortably, not too loosely or too tightly. If it's too tight, your puppy will choke as the animal grows; too loose, and he or she will easily paw or scratch at it and slip out.

Training Collars

When you're ready to train your dog, you'll need to decide the type of collar that is best and most effective for your dog and you. If you believe in the confrontational/aversive conditioning methods of training, you'll probably go to a choke or prong collar.

However, there's a growing movement toward more positive training, which we strongly support. Dr. Nicholas Dodman, director of the Tufts Behavior Clinic, believes that almost all dogs can and should be trained through positive reinforcement rather than inflicting pain. "Confrontational techniques, which grew out of World War II methods for training military animals, are outmoded and should be replaced by more motivational methods such as clicker and head-halter training," he says.

Whichever collar you choose for your dog, make sure the material is sturdy. Check the collar periodically to make sure it's not wearing out. Fatigue of the metal and material can happen and by checking your equipment frequently, you reduce the potential for dangerous escapes.

Consider a halter-type collar even for a pup. Proponents of positive dog training highly recommend these collars and since your dog is going to wiggle and squirm regardless of the style you select, you may want to consider adapting him or her to the halter style as a pup. They do cost more than a simple buckle collar—expect to pay anywhere from $10 to $50—and they require more adjustment.

Years ago, dogs were trained most often on chain-slip collars known as chokers. Today, the choices are much wider. The chain collar has been joined by a nylon version, snap-on slip collars, humane chokers, prong collars, head or halter collars, and remote or "shock" collars. Each training device has its followers—and some have strong opponents.

The simplest training collar is a **buckle collar**. The most common is the chain-slip collar or **"choke" collar**. Rising in popularity is the prong or **pinch collar**, a torturous-looking device that can be quite effective on boisterous dogs. The most appropriate option in our view is the halter or **head collar**, which fits the dog's whole head and uses the handler's ability to turn the dog's head rather than neck pressure as the control. The collar type that is best for you will depend a great deal on your dog's temperament. Whether he or she is submissive, dominant, or aggressive will be a key determinant as you select the type you're going to use.

Types of Collars

Buckle Collars

These collars consist of a simple loop of leather or nylon designed like a pants belt. They usually have expansion holes to accommodate growth. Although these can be found for five to ten dollars, you can go as elaborate as you like, with colors, fabrics, designs, glow-in-the-dark and even bells (no whistles as far as we know). These collars are not controversial. They're excellent everyday collars and inexpensive enough to replace frequently for a "new look." For training purposes, if you have a bright, eager-to-please pet, light tugs on these collars may be sufficient. Few of us are that lucky, however. With a buckle collar it is next to impossible to correct your dog if you favor physical correction. If you are using food rewards or clicker training methods, a buckle collar or a head halter will be all you'll ever need.

Chokers or Slip Collars

Slip collars come in metal or nylon. Metal slips more easily than nylon does, and can rub fur off the underside of the dog's neck more easily. The portion of the collar that rides on the top of the neck has a ring to which you attach the leash. The chain goes through the ring that is attached to the portion of the collar that goes under the dog's neck.

When purchasing a metal choke collar, you should ensure that the collar is smooth and slips freely. Choke collars work by tightening and loosening a noose around the dog's neck. Despite the

name, the idea is not to choke your dog. Instead, the premise behind these collars is that when a correction is warranted, a quick jerk and release will convince your dog to see things your way.

Choke collars should fit just below the dog's ears for the best results because this position delivers the sharpest correction. Do not use these collars in toy breeds. They are simply too dangerous for tiny dogs. Do not use them if you have to drag your dog along. Know that a hard jerk with a slip collar can damage a dog's trachea or even the spine in the neck region.

Slip collars are less effective in dogs with thick necks or thick coats, particularly if they slide out of position, because the physical discomfort they deliver under these circumstances is not as harsh and may not deliver the correction you seek.

Clip-On Nylon Training Collars

These collars sometimes are known as Volhard collars, named for the dog trainers that developed them. These slip collars are made of strong, lightweight nylon and feature a snap on one end, a floating ring, and a dead ring. Clip-on nylon collars are used like slip collars; the difference is that they come with a metal clip that prevents them from slipping down onto the dog's neck. The clip also eliminates the need to slip the collar over the dog's head.

This style collar offers great control because the collar stays right behind the ears, rather than on the heavily muscled neck area where collars generally ride. These collars tend to be stronger than chain chokers.

Prong Collars

Also called pinch collars, these have interlocking steel links, each with two blunt prongs that pinch the dog's skin when the collar is tightened. Sometimes the collars are put into a cloth tube (like a hair scrunchy). Although they look like medieval torture devices, prong

collars are popular tools among many trainers. However, we do not favor them because
we do not agree with the principle of using
pain to train. Like the choker, this collar is
used in a jerk and release manner. However,
the owner can deliver a sharper punishment
with less effort than with a choke collar.

The prong should not be used to train aggressive dogs and is too harsh for extremely
shy or fearful dogs. Also, *it is not appropriate for young puppies.* **The question is:
Should it be used at all?** Says Dr. Dodman,
"If you train a dog with positive methods,
you'll never need such a device."

Humane Chokers

Humane chokers look like prong collars made of chain instead of
interlocking links. The humane choker has two loops, one of which
fits around the dog's neck. The second loop is attached to the first
and is used to tighten the chain when necessary to guide the dog or
correct his behavior. This collar is becoming more popular among
trainers who prefer to teach the dog through motivation rather than
correction, which fits right in with the positive reinforcement, pre-
ferred method of training.

Shock or Remote Collars

These are easily the most controversial and expensive collars. They
consist of two parts: a transmitter that the owner or trainer has, and
a receiver that emits a minor shock to a buckle-type collar on the
dog. Manufacturers like to call them by the marketing-savvy de-
scription "remote collars," while critics prefer the term "shock" or
"E" for electric.

These collars have been around since the late 1950s. In the early
days of electric collars, they were used mostly as "no" collars by
hunters and hikers who liked to let their dogs roam while still ex-
ercising control over their activities. Today, they're more often used
as training tools.

Experts who recommend these collars say to use them only on
the most stubborn dogs. They recommend starting with the mildest
shock (equivalent to getting a static shock by walking across a car-
pet and touching something), and working up to a stronger strength,
only if necessary.

However, we believe that using shock for correction is simply

wrong and unnecessary. It is too easy to use these collars inappropriately, without the trainer being aware, and they can be sadistically abusive in the wrong hands.

The Shocking Truth

The Association of Pet Behaviour Counsellors (APBC) in England issued the following statement:

"The Association of Pet Behaviour Counsellors condemns the widespread use of devices that deliver electric shocks to dogs for the purpose of training or curing behaviour problems. Their potential for accidental misuse is high and they could easily cause considerable and unnecessary pain and distress to the animal.

"A dog experiencing an unpleasant shock to the neck 'out of the blue' will associate the sensation with what-ever the dog happens to be focusing on at the time. Used incorrectly, this could be an area, object, another dog, the owner or even a child. Unwanted side effects could easily occur when the dog being shocked becomes afraid of being in that area, or it could become afraid of, and as a result, potentially aggressive towards owners, children, other dogs or strangers.

"In inexperienced hands, it may take many repetitions of administrations of the shock before the punishment is finally associated with the unwanted behavior, and several more before the dog learns how to avoid the shock by performing the 'correct' action.

"Not only is this inhumane, but can set up a series of fears which can cause associated behavior problems in the future. In addition, it is possible that the device may be triggered by external influences, or malfunction, which may result in delivery of repeated shocks, particularly in those devices which are designed to be triggered by barking and are put onto dogs left alone for long periods.

"Only in a handful of cases, where all else has been tried and failed, and when the condition is potentially life-threatening, can the use of such devices ever be justified, and, only then, in the hands of an experienced behavioral specialist who is capable of accurate timing."

Head Collars or Harnesses

Head halters work by squeezing the dog's muzzle and putting pressure on the nape of the neck. They are also known as head harnesses and no-pull halters.

A harness is designed to distribute tension over a greater area of the dog's body, which is why they're the best choice for dogs who have injured tracheas or cervical areas and for toy breeds. The head collar or halter has two basic parts: the collar that fits snugly around the dog's neck just in back of the ears, and the face loop that fits loosely over the muzzle and allows complete and gentle control of the head.

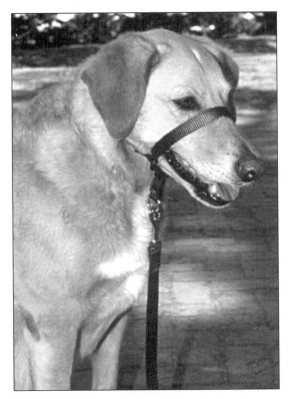

A self-correcting head halter is an effective alternative to more punitive training collars. If your dog charges ahead of you, the leash tightens, the halter directs the dog's head and shoulders back toward you, and the rest of the body follows.

The face loop is not a muzzle. The dog can breathe, pant, eat, drink, and kiss your face while wearing the face loop. The leash is attached to the head collar underneath the dog's snout.

Most dogs fight the head collar at first but, if the equipment is fitted correctly, they quickly become used to it. To help your dog adjust, you may want to provide treats when he or she walks without pawing at the face loop, and calmly control the animal if he or she tries to remove the loop.

Since the leash is attached to the head collar, gentle pressure upward on the leash will stop the dog from pawing at the loop. If your dog drops his or her head to paw at the loop, just lift up and keep walking. If the dog forges ahead, steady pressure on the leash will turn the animal back toward you.

■ Head collars do a better job of stopping a pushy puller than other types of products on the market.

■ Head collars work because they lead the dog from the head, where the animal lacks the strength and leverage to be able to pull. A dog who tries to pull while wearing a head collar simply has his or her head turned gently back toward the handler.

Although some high-strung dogs never learn to tolerate wearing something on their head and face, and some need a period of adjustment before they accept them, head collars are the most effective and humane no-pull aid for most dogs. For further discussion, please see Chapter 16, "Head Collars."

Also, please note that these product evaluations were conducted independent of Tufts University School of Veterinary Medicine and their inclusion in this book is not an endorsement by Tufts.

Body Harnesses

Body harnesses are often used on draft dogs to facilitate pulling sleds or carts. They're also used to signal police and guide dogs that it's time for work. Harnesses encourage a dog to move in front of the handler, which is useful for working dogs but counterproductive for casual strolls in the park. The principle: when the dog pulls on the leash, the harness tightens around the dog, causing a low level of discomfort. When the dog stops pulling, the discomfort stops, so the dog is rewarded for not pulling. We asked a consulting trainer to evaluate two brands of no-pull harnesses.

Holt Control Harness

The Holt Harness is made of soft, braided nylon with sturdy hardware. An elasticized band cushions the chest to minimize rubbing. Though confusing to put on the dog the first time, once you figure it out the harness is simple to use.

Our consulting trainer tested this device on several dogs and found that tolerance and effectiveness was high. Unlike the head collar, most dogs did not need a time to become acclimated to the harness. Four out of six shelter dogs tested (of various sizes and temperaments) responded well and immediately reduced their pulling. But a stressed and hyperactive Rottweiler barely seemed to notice the harness, and the last dog, a wiry terrier mix, almost managed to escape the harness. He was effectively stopped from pulling, but minutes later, changed his tactics to include spinning and trying to grab the leash snapped to the harness. This tack was successful for him; the harness affords precious little ability to control a dog unless he or she pulls straight away from the handler, and the terrier's playful, exuberant spinning and jumping quickly got him tangled up. If your dog is a straight-away, enthusiastic puller, this product would probably work really well.

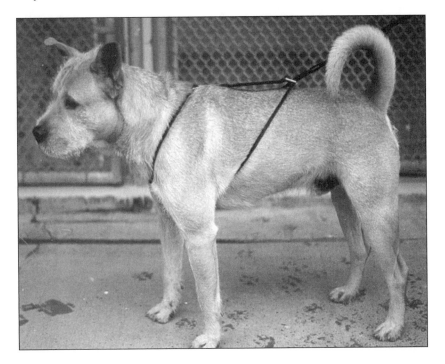

Pro-Stop! Harness

This harness works on a principle similar to that of the Holt, but with a twist. Here, the corrective tightening comes from padded leg straps wrapped around the dog's front legs instead of around the chest. The location of the straps (above the dog's front elbows, high in the armpits) appears very uncomfortable for any dog, even if the animal isn't pulling against his or her restraint.

This product was more effective than the Holt Harness on our Rottweiler, but a sweet Australian Shepherd and a submissive black Labrador were befuddled by the pressure on their legs. Sensitive dogs might get too distracted to enjoy a walk while wearing this harness and may even injure themselves.

SENSE-ation Harness

Relatively new on the market, this harness has received numerous positive reviews. It applies horse training concepts and comes with a training guide. The harness consists of a nylon loop just behind the dog's front legs and a connecting strap across the dog's chest.

The Right Choice

Any collar, but particularly a choke collar, is potentially dangerous if left on an unsupervised dog. The very design of the choke collar makes it easier for dogs to strangle themselves, since the dangling ring can catch on objects, causing the dog to panic and hang him or herself.

The design of both the buckle and pinch collars make it more difficult to catch the rings on objects. Neither the pinch collar nor the buckle collar is designed to tighten in the way that the choke does. Still, be aware that if a dog catches the collar, the dog can strangle, no matter what kind of collar the animal is wearing. So, which is the best collar? It's the one with which you get the type of cooperation you want from your dog.

You should be able to control and work with your dog without constantly "reminding" the animal what to do. Nagging a dog on a choke collar, or any collar, should indicate to you that your dog is ignoring your corrections. In essence, you are effectively training the dog to ignore you—just as a human being would in the same "nagging" situation. Continuous jerking, whether in a buckle or slip collar, hints that another type of collar, training method, or tool should be implemented.

We favor the head harness because it fits in with a positive-reinforcement style of training. Says Dr. Dodman: "If we can train a killer whale to launch itself out of a swimming pool, roll on its side and urinate in a small plastic cup with a whistle and a bucket of fish as a reward, we should be able to train a domestic dog to do anything you want to with equivalent positive reinforcement." Have you ever seen a trainer at Sea World *spank* a dolphin?

The bottom line should be to use the *mildest* collar that gives the results you need. If that's a simple, inexpensive buckle collar or a halter, you are far, far ahead of the game. Dr. Dodman says, "If you use the right reward for the right dog, and it isn't always food, you will have a dog who will respond over 85 percent of the time, which is all the average domestic dog ever needs. If people use collars suitable for positive training, such as halters, they're going to have happier dogs, and they'll be happier owners as well."

Collar Savvy

■ ***Preventing Dependence:*** *No matter what type of training collar you select, try to make sure your dog doesn't become dependent on it. Dogs associate a learned behavior (such as walking calmly by your side) with the device used during the learning process. Thus, if you replace a training collar with an everyday collar, your dog may pull once again.*

You can avoid "device dependence" by always rewarding your dog for appropriate behavior and by gradually weaning your dog off the training collar.

■ ***Appropriate Fit:*** *Proper fit is important with any collar. When dogs wear buckle collars too loosely, they can back out of them. To prevent this, keep the collar tight enough that you can fit only two fingers comfortably* *underneath it. Choke collars are most effective when worn high on the neck, right behind the ears. Always follow manufacturer's instructions when fitting head halters and body harnesses.*

■ ***On or Off?*** *While it's advisable for your dog to wear a collar most of the time, there are times when the animal is better off without neckwear.*

Because choke and buckle collars can snag and strangle a dog, consider removing such collars when your dog is inside the house or in your fenced yard. And remove any collar or halter when your dog is in a crate.

Lowdown on Leashes

Leashes present fewer choices than collars, and there are fewer professional differences of opinion about them.Generally, a six-foot leash is best for training or routine walks. Longer leads are useful for outdoor training—especially when teaching the "come" command. But be aware that in some communities a dog is considered "at large" if it's at the end of a leash longer than six feet.

Canvas or leather leashes are easiest on your hands. Make sure the clip is strong, but not so big that it slaps your dog while walking. Retractable leashes are increasingly popular, but their long length and extendibility encourage pulling. And, getting tangled in the thin cord can injure a dog or the handler.

Remember, dog tack is a management tool, not a crutch. Nothing works better than praise and kindness to encourage your dog to stay by your side. The ultimate goal is to have your dog focused on you—not on what's around his or her neck.

Dogs who strain at their leashes (and who subsequently get jerked by their frustrated handlers) are more likely to have spinal misalignments, and dogs with spinal problems have a much higher incidence of aggressive and/or hyperactive behavior problems.

Another Solution

Dennis Fetko, a San Diego-based dog trainer and applied animal behaviorist, advocates a simple way to cure dogs of pulling on lead. The method works with any type of collar (though he prefers a close-fitting nylon slip collar) and doesn't involve any jerking or tugging.

"Whenever you feel tension on the lead from your dog pulling, stop dead in your tracks," advises Dr. Fetko. Don't move until your dog turns around or backs up to put slack back in the leash. Only then should you praise your dog and continue walking. "Your dog will learn quickly that a slack leash, not pulling, will get it what it wants—forward progress." ■

16

Head Collars

The head collar works on dogs just like a halter works on horses. It's a smart, gentle way to alter your dog's troubling behavior.

You see it in group classes with dogs and puppies alike. More than half the animals arrive pulling and lunging so hard that they choke themselves and yank their owners around. And it isn't just the big breeds: West Highland Terriers gag and strangle themselves, and Miniature Dachshunds pull so hard that their paws are raw.

This condition tends to worsen over time. Taking the dog for a walk becomes less and less enjoyable for the human at the end of the leash, resulting in less frequent and shorter walks. The problem is compounded when the dog walker has a back, shoulder, or elbow problem or arthritis. Walking an out-of-control dog is not only unpleasant for these people, but it is dangerous as well.

A Practical Solution

The solution is called a head collar, and it works on dogs like a halter works on horses. Head collars have a strap that fits over the nose of the dog, so that you lead from the head, not the neck. Just as with bigger, stronger animals like horses or bulls, by controlling the head, you control the whole dog.

At first glance, the loop that fits over the dog's nose may give the appearance of a muzzle. Actually, the loop allows dogs the freedom to open their mouths to eat, drink, pant, even carry a toy. As long as the animals maintain a loose leash, they are free to open their mouths. But if they try to pull, or lunge, or bite, the head collar turns the dogs' head, preventing the problem. And, the person on the other end of the leash doesn't have to pull hard to achieve this effect! In most cases, even young children or elderly people can lead large dogs who were previously unmanageable. It takes much less effort to control the nose of the dog than to control the powerful neck muscles.

A training priority is to use methods that are fun and non-aggressive so that the dog receives positive input. The tendency for many people when using choke chains or pinch collars is to constantly tug and yank on their dogs. Over time, the dogs learn to ignore the signal. Even when used as designed, choke chains and pinch collars inflict pain to control behavior. Yanking on pinch collars and choke chains when a dog is aggressive around other people or dogs only adds to the negative experience. And, suppressing this behavior through painful means does not change the dog's attitude.

With a head collar, however, the correction for pulling isn't pain, but displacement. Every time the dog tries to pull away, his or her head is turned back toward the handler. The dog cannot lean into or overwhelm the strength of the person holding the leash. Under these circumstances, most dogs immediately cease pulling.

Is your dog yanking your chain? Try a head collar.

That doesn't mean head collars are a panacea. They should never be used for tying up a dog or for constant wear. They are strictly for training, and should be removed promptly when the dog's training or exercise session is completed.

But if owners realize they can walk their dogs without a struggle, they will walk them more often, resulting in better behavior both on the walks and at home. Going for regular walks helps dogs burn off excess energy and is a great way for dogs and people to form stronger bonds. Walking also gives you an opportunity to introduce your dog to lots of new sights and sounds and teach him or her appropriate behavior.

> *“ JUST AS WITH BIGGER, STRONGER ANIMALS LIKE HORSES OR BULLS, BY CONTROLLING THE HEAD, YOU CONTROL THE WHOLE DOG. ”*

Battle-tested

The first night of any beginning level dog training class can be chaotic. For many people, this is their first time in a group class and often with their first dog. Owners get dragged through the parking lot. Dogs bark and lunge at other dogs. Owners' faces reflect utter relief and amazement after their dogs are fitted with head collars. Within five minutes, the dogs are calm, quiet, and under control.

The head collar also allows you to teach a dog to behave in distracting situations. Exposing a dog to different stimulating situations helps him or her learn to calm down and walk without pulling. Many dogs are able to return to wearing a regular buckle collar after just a few months of learning how to control themselves with the head collar.

How to Fit Your Dog's Head Collar

Using a head collar to control your dog's head and mouth enables you to keep even the most excitable animal under control without causing any pain. However, if your dog is aggressive toward people or other dogs, fitting a head collar may trigger an undesirable response. Contact a qualified trainer or behaviorist to assist you.

When properly introduced, it only takes few minutes or, at most, a couple of short sessions for the dog to accept a head collar. Proper fit is very important for comfort and for your dog's acceptance of the head collar. It should fit comfortably without restricting use of the mouth when the leash is loose.

When putting a head collar on a dog for the first time, offer a yummy treat as he or she pokes his head through the loop. Your dog will quickly see that he or she has full use of the mouth for eating, and the treat will give some incentive for accepting the head collar the next time.

Right after putting on the head collar, distract the dog while he or she adjusts to the way the equipment feels. Then, take the dog for a short walk. If the animal continues to struggle, encourage him or her to walk beside you by patting your leg and with verbal encouragement. It is helpful to use treats to get your pet to stay near your side as you walk.

This allows the dog to learn that if he or she maintains slack in the leash, the head collar remains open and the freedom of the leash leash may be explored.

Choosing the Right Head Collar

Following are evaluations of three styles of head collars. Although the designs differ, the concept of leading from the head is the same. While each has its advantages due to subtle design differences, ultimately the success of each depends on how well it fits the shape of the dog's head and nose.

Also, please note that these product evaluations were conducted independent of Tufts University School of Veterinary Medicine and their inclusion in this book is not an endorsement by Tufts.

Gentle Leader

The Gentle Leader was developed by Dr. R. K. Anderson, a retired director of the Animal Behavior Clinic at the University of Minnesota, and Dr. Ruth Foster, past president of the National Association of Dog Obedience Instructors. For some time, this head collar was available only through dog trainers and veterinarians,  but it now also is sold in pet stores.

Of the three models evaluated here, the Gentle Leader is the only one without side straps. That means once you adjust the head collar, it moves around on the dog's head less than the other two models, which is good for sensitive dogs, since the simpler design gives them less collar of which to be aware. The proper fit of the nose loop is dependent on the proper fit of the neck strap. Note that the tightening action of the nose loop is distracting to some dogs, and is unnecessary to teach most dogs to stop pulling.

Snoot Loop

The Snoot Loop was developed by Peter L. Borchelt, an applied animal behaviorist and the director of the Animal Behavior Clinic at the Animal Medical Center in New York.

The Snoot Loop's design makes it the easiest head collar to adjust for fit. Its side straps connecting the neck loop and the nose loop are adjustable, making it easier to fit dogs that have a big head and a short "snoot."

The petite size is the answer for hard-to-fit toy breeds such as Yorkshire Terriers and Miniature Pinschers. Dr. Borchelt has another Snoot Loop designed especially for breeds such as the Pug and Bulldog. And, if you purchase a Snoot Loop that cannot be adjusted to fit correctly, the company will custom-make one to fit.

The Snoot Loop's straps are made out of the narrowest material of the three head collars. This means that when a dog pulls against straps, the pressure exerted on the dog's nose is sharper than the pressure exerted by the wider straps of the other two brands. The loose weave of the material makes the threads apt to snag if the dog paws at the head collar.

Halti

The Halti head collar was designed by Dr. Roger Mugford in England. Like the Snoot Loop, the Halti has side straps that improve the fit of the head collar, but the Halti's side straps are not adjustable. Both the nylon material and the hardware (metal rings) of the Halti are sturdier than that of the Snoot Loop, however. ■

Head Collar How-To

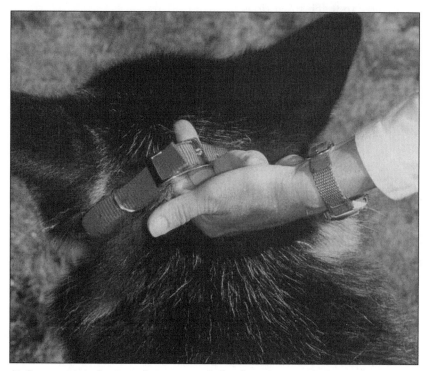

Before putting the nose loop around the dog's nose, get the neck strap fitted correctly. Without using the nose loop, fasten and adjust this strap so that it is high and snug, close behind the dog's ears. It should be tight enough that only one finger can fit between the strap and the dog.

Next, take the neck strap off, and teach your dog to put his or her nose through the nose loop. Offer a treat as this is done. Then fasten the neck strap, which is already adjusted to the correct tightness. Distract the dog with a little play after you fasten the head collar.

Head Collar How-To

Head collars work by turning the dog's head in your direction when you gently pull on the leash. With a properly adjusted head collar, you will never have to yank or pull hard. The nose loop of the Gentle Leader has an adjustment under the dog's jaw. The nose loop should slide from just underneath the dog's eyes almost to the tip of his or her nose. With adult dogs, you only have to adjust the straps the first time you use the head collar. But with growing puppies, check the fit every time it's used.

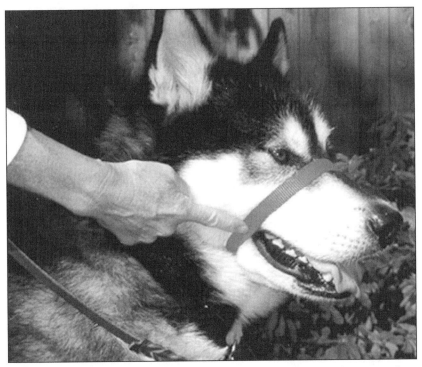

The nose loop should cross just behind the corner of the mouth so your dog has full use of his or her mouth.

20

Electronic Fences

An old-fashioned, solid fence,
good training and sufficient exercise
are still the best bets.

With more than ten years' field experience under his belt, the humane officer from Santa Clara County, California, thought he had seen and heard just about everything. Then he got the call from a hysterical woman who had come home from work to find that her dog was being shocked nonstop by his electronic collar.

"Please hurry!" she begged. "He's totally crazed, and when we try to touch him, we get shocked. We can't get the collar off him!"

The officer rushed to the scene. When he arrived he found that the owners had managed to throw a rug over the dog, restrain him, and cut off the offending collar with a knife. The dog was still so severely traumatized by the experience that he refused to allow anyone to come near him. The woman vowed never to use her underground fence system again.

Electronic fences and their partners—collars that deliver an aversive agent—have been around for more than twenty years. They seem like the perfect canine confinement alternative to a solid physical fence. They are often marketed as the ideal fencing solution to homeowner association fence prohibitions and for problematic, difficult-to-fence, steep, rocky, and rugged living spaces.

But while occurrences such as the one described above are relatively rare, there are other drawbacks to using electronic fencing systems. A conscientious owner will weigh all the pros and cons before deciding whether or not to invest in this sort of system.

How Do They Work?

Electronic fences rely on the transmission of a radio signal from a wire or some other transmitter that is typically buried or mounted in an unobtrusive location on the dog owner's property. The radio signal is broadcast within a specific zone, following the contours of the individual layout. The dog wears a battery-operated receiver on a special collar, which picks up the radio signals when the dog enters the special zone. Most of the systems are programmed so that a "warning tone" is emitted when the dog first approaches the radio transmission area, and, if he or she remains or travels further into the zone, follows up with an aversive stimulus.

The most commonly used aversive is an electric shock, delivered to the dog's neck by metal (electrically conducting) prongs set in the collar. A recent technological innovation provides for some systems to deliver a burst of citronella spray as the aversive instead of an electric shock.

The best of the electronic fence makers teach the dog owners how to condition their dogs to the fence. "Training flags" are installed around the perimeter of the dog's "safe" territory, to give him or her a visual reminder of its shape and size. For the first few days, it is suggested that the owner apply tape over the prongs on the electrical collar to minimize any shock that the dog receives, and to keep the dog on a leash. The owner is instructed to walk around the property, allowing the dog to approach the forbidden zones and hear the warning tone. The owner is to pull or call the dog back into the safe area, and then praise the dog.

The next phase involves removing the tape and allowing the dog (who is still on a leash) farther into the danger zone, where he or she experiences a correction. Again, the owner brings the dog back into the safety zone, praising the retreat from the forbidden area. This is followed by a few more days of off-leash but supervised experiences and, finally, removal of the training flags. Whether the aversive is a shock or spray, in most cases it takes only a few applications for the dog to learn that the tone means "Bad things happen here."

Advantages of "Virtual" Fences

There are certainly advantages to electronic fences. They are generally less expensive than a physical fence. Systems range in cost from 120 to 400 dollars, and can cover terrain ranging from a small yard to a 100-acre parcel, depending on the brand. Variation in cost depends in large part on the features included in the system package, such as adjustable levels of shock strength, rechargeable batteries, and combination fence and no-bark or fence and remote trainer systems. If you are considering investing in an electronic fence, compare features carefully to get the brand that best suits your needs.

Electronic fences also are easier to install than a traditional fence. One system uses a wire that is buried a few inches underground, a process that is much less labor-intensive than digging post holes and building fences, especially in rocky soil or on steep brushy slopes. Another type of fence doesn't even require a buried wire, but instead uses transmitters on "emitter posts" that are inserted into the ground at intervals around the property. Consumers can install the fences themselves, or hire one of the many landscapers and builders who have experience in underground fence installation. Some companies will provide a list of certified fence installers on request.

For those who simply prefer the aesthetics of a fenceless yard or are faced with homeowner association constraints, electronic fences can keep a dog contained without obstructing the view or violating neighborhood sensibilities.

The Negative Side

Paul Miller was the Santa Clara humane officer who responded to the call of a dog being shocked by his collar a decade ago. Ten more years of experience in the field haven't softened his opinion of the product. He argues that electronic fences don't provide adequate containment to reasonably guarantee a dog's safety.

"I can't tell you exactly how many stray dogs I've seen wearing electronic fence collars," he says, "but it's a lot. Owners forget to replace weak and dying batteries and dogs are soon free to come and go at will. Many owners who come in to shelters to retrieve their shock-collared wayward hounds will admit that they were aware the batteries were weak and they hadn't bothered to replace them."

Another minus: some dogs seem to have no trouble braving the strong corrections imposed on them by a working collar with fresh batteries if they are presented with sufficiently enticing stimuli: a female in season, a fast-moving cat, a child on a bicycle, a postal worker. And then the dog is stuck outside the fence without sufficient motivation to risk the shock to get back in! For this reason, certain breeds, especially large dogs bred for guardian jobs or dogs with strong hunting drives, make poor candidates for these systems.

Another important consideration is the fact that an electronic fence does nothing to protect your dog from outside harm. The neighborhood canine bully can still enter your yard and attack your dog. Bad people can still come onto your property and steal or torment your dog. (We've even heard one report of an expensive electronic collar being stolen right off a dog!) Also, these electronic fences don't keep children or delivery people from approaching your house and being attacked or bitten by your dog.

Finally, dogs with especially long or thick coats may have to have their necks shaved for the prongs (and the corrective shocks) to reach their skin. Such disfigurement is not acceptable to all owners.

"Mild" Is a Matter of Opinion

Dog owners also need to be concerned about the unintended negative side effects of punishment. Despite the euphemisms used in promotional materials that call the aversive electric shock a "mild electrical stimulus," a "stimulus distraction," a "tingle," or a "tickle," it is, in fact, an electric shock.

In November 1998 at the Association of Pet Dog Trainers annual conference and trade show in Valley Forge, Pennsylvania, a number of dog trainers tested an electric collar by wrapping it around their own hands. The equipment was provided by one of the electronic fence manufacturers, who had a trade booth at the convention. People reacted to varying levels of shock with significantly different levels of sensitivity. While some felt nothing at the lowest setting and only a mild sensation at level three, others described a mildly painful sensation at level one and unpleasant, even intolerable pain at the higher settings. (The shock was felt on the hand, not on the more sensitive neck area. Product representatives refused to allow the human guinea pigs to test the collars on their necks.) There is every reason to think that our dogs would also have different sensitivities to electric shocks.

The use of punishment in training, especially a punishment as intense as an electric shock, risks irreparable harm to the mutual trust that is critically important in the dog-human relationship. During the training process, the dog may associate the shock or spray with the owner's presence and end up fearing the owner.

Sensitive dogs can be seriously traumatized by just one administration of the punishing aversive. Some dogs may refuse to enter the yard at all after being shocked or sprayed, especially if the yard is small, with a limited amount of "free" space where the dog can feel safe. One Monterey County, California dog owner reports that while she loves the electronic fence system because it allows her dogs to run loose on her several-acre property (which she couldn't otherwise afford to fence), her Komondor is so respectful of the boundary that the dog won't cross it even when not wearing the collar. The owner has to load her dog into the car and drive across the wire just to take the dog for a walk around the neighborhood.

> 66 THERE IS NOTHING THAT CAN REPLACE TRAINING, SUPERVISION, AND A PURELY "VISIBLE," SOLID, WELL-MAINTAINED FENCE. 99

What Are the Alternatives?

What are you supposed to do if you live in an area where fencing is prohibited, prohibitively expensive, or simply not feasible? You can keep your dog in the house, train him or her to come when called, and allow the animal outside only under direct supervision. You can install a cable runner, although tying a dog up creates its own set of risks and problems. You can purchase a chain-link kennel run to provide safe confinement for your dog when you aren't able to personally supervise his or her exercise. Or you can move to a neighborhood that allows physical fences.

Some people, however, feel the benefits of an electronic fence system outweigh the negatives of the alternatives. We'd grudgingly acknowledge the potential usefulness of the system, provided it's used in the following limited circumstances.

Because of the potential for an electronic fence to malfunction, for your dog to simply "run through" it and escape, and for predators to enter your property and injure your dog, we suggest using the system only when you are home and able to monitor its use. This means not using the system when you are not at home (even just for a few minutes), or at night (or any other time you may be sleeping). You must check on your dog constantly, establishing visual contact at least every five minutes or so when he or she is "confined" by the fence and nothing else. And the collar must be removed whenever the fence is not being used as the primary barrier (when the dog is safely confined in the house, for instance). Failing to do all these things exposes the dog to the dangers discussed above, while simultaneously giving the owner a false sense of security.

Of course, if your dog is reliably trained to come to you when called and you are keeping him or her under this sort of close supervision, you probably don't need this sort of system! And that fact strikes at the heart of our objections to electronic fences: they are really designed as a "convenience" device for people who like having dogs and don't want them to run away, but who are unwilling or unable to go the extra mile to absolutely ensure the safety of their animals.

There are exceptions. There are dog owners, for instance, who keep their well-trained dogs under close supervision, but who maintain the electronic fence as a sort of emergency back-up barrier for their dogs because they live on a busy road, and even an extremely rare, quick trip off the property could result in death.

In our opinion, there is nothing that can replace training, supervision, and that timeless tool for good neighbors everywhere: a purely "visible," solid, well-maintained fence. ■

18

Training Beyond the Basics

*Training can be more than just
endless drills. New methods and goals
provide fun for dogs and owners alike.*

Not so very long ago, trainers assumed that anyone who signed up for a basic obedience class was seeking that perfectly straight sit position. Classes were conducted with military precision, trainers barking commands as owners marched their dogs in a circle, jerking and popping on leashes and choke chains to achieve lightning-fast responses. Success was measured by speed and perfection of position, and advanced work was conducted with one goal—to show in American Kennel Club obedience competitions, earn obedience degrees, and achieve scores as close to that magic "perfect 200" as possible.

A New Training Paradigm

My, how the times have changed! A relatively few years ago, many trainers began to realize that the greater percentage of dog owners in their classes really only wanted a well-behaved companion—a trustworthy family dog. Who cared if the dog was sitting three degrees off perfect? Most owners were just happy the dog sat at all, and couldn't have cared less about scores in the obedience ring. Thus began a paradigm shift in the dog training world, from obedience competition training to family dog training. With that shift has come an exciting vista of advanced training opportunities and breathtakingly fun dog-related activities.

Untapped Skills

All of our dogs are capable of doing far more than we ask of them. Their senses, especially hearing and olfactory, are so highly developed that they can perform feats that appear miraculous. Their physical abilities are awesome, as demonstrated by the prowess of highly skilled Frisbee and agility dogs. And they have talents that reveal the versatility and breadth of their potential to think, reason, and learn—if only we tap into those talents.

Today, there are more possibilities for canine recreational activities than ever. Mixed breed dogs, once second-class citizens in training classes, can now compete in obedience through the American Mixed Breed Obedience Registry (AMBOR) or the Mixed Breed Dog Club and at national obedience competitions. They can also join their blue-blooded brothers and sisters in agility, herding, flyball, Frisbee, tracking, drill team, square dancing, musical freestyle, the My Dog Can Do That board game, the Canine Good Citizen Programs, animal-assisted therapy programs, tricks classes, lure coursing, (take a breath) television, advertising, movie work, water dog sports.... There is something out there for every dog's talents.

> ❝ IF YOU HAVEN'T DISCOVERED YOUR DOG'S HIDDEN TALENTS, PERHAPS YOU'RE NOT LOOKING, OR YOU NEED TO CULTIVATE HIS OR HER CREATIVITY. ❞

Developing Your Dog's Potential

Dogs who are encouraged to engage in activities that stimulate them mentally and draw upon their innate talents are less frustrated and better behaved than their less fortunate littermates who languish, bored and lonely, in their backyards. Owners whose dogs are less frustrated and better behaved can appreciate their dogs more, enjoy engaging in activities with them, and are more likely to fulfill their social contract to provide a lifelong loving home for their canine companions. The new, non-competition-based classes that rely primarily on the use of positive training methods are the best approach to developing a dog with acceptable social skills while building an unbreakable bond between canine and human.

Discover the Talent!

If you haven't discovered your dog's hidden talents, perhaps you're not looking, or you need to cultivate his or her creativity. Here's how you can encourage your dog to develop his or her full potential for amazing behaviors:

■ **Spend more time with your dog.** To uncover your dog's hidden talents, you have to have a relationship with this animal. Dogs who live in the backyard twenty-four hours a day may have all kinds of talents, but you will never know. The more time you spend with your dog, the more likely you are to notice his or her astounding abilities.

■ **Encourage spontaneous behaviors.** If you are on the lookout for talent, you are more likely to spot it when it occurs. If you have conditioned your dog to a reward marker (the click! of a clicker or a verbal "Yes!" that tells your dog a treat is coming), you can mark and reward the animal when he or she does something cute, useful or creative that you would like to have repeated. You will be surprised how quickly your dog can learn to deliberately offer behaviors that you capture with a click!

■ **Consider your dog's genes.** Scent hounds are bred to follow their noses. Chances are good that your beagle or Basset Hound's hidden talents might lie in the tracking field. Golden retrievers, Labradors, and the herding breeds tend to have a natural aptitude for retrieving, thanks to decades of genetic selection for bringing back waterfowl, game birds, and sheep.

If you know the skills for which your dog was bred, you know where to start looking for talent. Don't limit yourself to the genetic predisposition, however—plenty of dogs' talents lie far afield of their genetically selected behaviors.

■ **Provide learning opportunities.** The more you expose your dog to different environments and new stimuli, the more likely you are to discover those hidden talents.

■ **Set your dog up to succeed.** Manage the environment so he or she can experiment and explore without getting into trouble. The more the dog is punished for trying new things, the more he or she is likely to shut down and stick with tried and true, safe behaviors. We want the dog to offer new behaviors so we can reward them.

For instance, if we want to encourage retrieving, we must make sure we don't leave shoes, books, and kids' toys where the dog can get them, then yell at him or her for picking them up. The more often this dog is punished for picking up inappropriate items, the more likely we are to destroy any interest in retrieving. The more we reward him or her for picking things up, the more we reinforce the retrieving behavior.

Of course, not all hidden talents are useful. Some, such as opening the refrigerator and snitching the chicken, can be annoying or, worse, dangerous. While we may admire dogs' ingenuity, we also need to stop them from hurting themselves or destroying valuable possessions. In cases like this, it is often easier to prevent or manage the behavior than to retrain it. It is simpler to install a latch on the refrigerator door than to set up complicated booby traps to extinguish a behavior that your dog has found exceptionally rewarding. Restricting access by closing doors, putting valuables in a safe place, or using crates, pens or leashes, can go a long way toward extinguishing unwanted talents without stifling canine creativity.

Basic Training—The Foundation

Basic training is the foundation for any of the more advanced canine activities. If you are interested in pursuing the less formal doggie activities, you can start by finding a basic class whose trainer is more interested in making sure the students—both two- and four-legged—have a good time while they learn than in maintaining strict discipline in the canine classroom. Once you have graduated from a basic training class, you are ready to explore the big wide world of more advanced canine activities. Here are several of the many activities now available in most parts of the country. See this book's appendix for more information.

My Dog Can Do That
A board game you play with your dog—whoever heard of such a thing? These days, more and more dog owners have, as word spreads about My Dog Can Do That. This delightful game requires the use

of positive reinforcement training methods. Owners pick cards from any one of three decks, at three different levels of difficulty. Each card describes a "trick" or behavior that the dog has to do. Examples of each level of difficulty are:

- **Beginner:** Dog sits still while player skips ten feet away and stops.

- **Intermediate:** Dog lays down, rolls over, then stand up.

- **Advanced:** Dog retrieves a toy and drops it in a basket five feet from the player.

Owners can use treats, praise, hand signals, and other verbal or body language cues as needed, but no anger or force, and no pushing, pulling, jerking, or yelling. You can play it as a family game, with each person taking turns drawing a card and working with the dog. Or, you and your dog can play against your friends and their dogs. Or you can take part in the increasing number of matches and tournaments that are being held around the country.

Be forewarned—dog owners who are serious about this game are practicing all of the behaviors on the cards with their dogs. You'd better hurry if you want to catch up! Animal shelters and training clubs are starting to offer MDCDT competitions as fundraisers.

Agility

It's an obstacle course for dogs, complete with tunnels, jumps, a teeter-totter, and several other items to challenge your dog's agility. Dogs of all shapes and sizes love it—experienced dogs run an entire course by themselves while the owner stands in the middle of the ring. Three of the four organizations that sponsor competitions welcome mixed-breed participation, so there's no excuse—anyone can play!

Flyball

You have to see this one to believe it. Flyball is a hurdle relay race for a team of four dogs of any heritage. Each dog in turn jumps four jumps, spaced ten feet apart. At the end of the jumps is a flyball box. When the dog touches the pedal on the front of the box, a tennis ball shoots out. The dog catches the ball and goes back over the four jumps to the owner waiting at the starting line. Then the next dog goes. The team that finishes first wins. Flyball is a very competitive sport, and great fun to watch. Dogs with an affinity for retrieving tennis balls adore this game.

Herding

When you think of sheep or cattle dogs, you tend to visualize Australian Shepherds and Border Collies. But the list of dogs who can be taught to herd includes multipurpose breeds with herding ancestors way back in their bloodlines, and  mixed-breed dogs with some herding blood. And the list of breeds that are officially designated as herding dogs is much longer than most people think—some thirty breeds, including the Rottweiler, Tibetan Terrier and the Samoyed. Multipurpose dogs who can herd comprise another dozen or so, including such unlikely breeds as the Kerry Blue Terrier, Poodle, Soft Coated Wheaten Terrier, and Schipperke.

Herding is the perfect outlet for the high-energy Border Collie and the other intense herding breeds, as it makes full use of their extreme intelligence and obsessive herding behaviors.

Musical Freestyle

Affectionately known as "Dancing With Dogs," musical or canine freestyle is most akin to a combination of ballroom dancing and pairs figure skating. People and dogs dance together to music of the person's choosing, in a routine choreographed to suit the dog's personality and abilities The routine can range from short and simple to long and complex.

Animal-Assisted Therapy

Therapy dogs can be any breed, mix, size, shape, or color, as long as they are well behaved; can tolerate disturbing events like rolling wheelchairs, falling crutches, and patients who don't always behave like other people; and enjoy being the center of attention.

There are national organizations that provide certification for therapy dogs, and many local humane societies offer therapy programs. These programs always welcome new volunteers because the demand for animal-assisted therapy is so high.

Imagine how it would feel to be deprived, long term—maybe forever—of the touch of your dog's soft fur or the caress of his or her tongue. The human handlers speak of miracles among non-responsive patients who move, even speak, for the first time in months when a therapy dog greets them and of faces that light up when a furry friend arrives.

Frisbee

We've all watched them in awe—on beaches, in parks, and during halftime at football games—those incredibly athletic dogs who leap eight feet off the ground and catch a Frisbee in midair. Frisbee is an activity you don't even have to go to a class to learn. All you need is a dog who loves to jump and retrieve and, of course, a Frisbee. Even dogs who aren't naturals at the game can learn to play Frisbee, and there are loads of resources—books, Frisbee clubs, and Web sites. For those who want to get serious about this, there are canine Frisbee competitions almost everywhere, including national championships. Be sure to have your veterinarian okay your dog's participation in this activity.

Tracking

A tracking dog follows the scent trail left by a human being (or other animal) who has passed along a particular route. Tracking can be done as a hobby (for fun), as a sport (to earn titles), as part of a serious effort to save human and animal lives through search-and-rescue work, and in law enforcement.
The ability of a dog to follow scent trails that are "invisible" to the human nose seems uncanny, but we all know that a canine nose is thousands of times more sensitive than a human nose. ■

Appendix

Editor's Note: This list of organizations, books, products and other information is by no means exhaustive. It provides a sampling of resources of interest to dog owners as this book went to press. Web and mailing addresses and phone numbers change frequently.

No specific ordering information is listed for products generally available at online and bricks and mortar bookstores and pet care stores.

Finally, products are listed here as a reader service. Their inclusion is not an endorsement by Tufts University School of Veterinary Medicine.

Agility

American Kennel Club (AKC)
5580 Centerview Dr.
Raleigh, NC 27606
(919) 233-9767
www.akc.org

**North American
Dog Agility Council**
11522 South Hwy. 3
Cataldo, ID 83810
www.nadac.com

United Kennel Club
100 E. Kilgore Rd.
Kalamazoo, MI 49001
(269) 343-9020
www.ukcdogs.com

U. S. Dog Agility Association
P.O. Box 850955
Richardson, TX 75085-0955
(972) 487-2200
www.usdaa.com

Disc Play

**Hyperflite Skyhoundz
Canine Disc Championships**
1015C Collier Rd.
Atlanta, GA 30318
(404) 350-9343
www.skyhoundz.com

**International Disc Dog
Handlers' Association**
1690 Julius Bridge Rd.
Ball Ground, GA 30107
(770)735-6200
www.iddha.com

Herding

**American Herding
Breed Association**
www.ahba-herding.org

AKC Test/Trial Program
51 Madison Ave.
New York, NY 10010
www.akc.org

Australian Shepherd Club of America
P.O. Box 3790
Bryan, TX 77803-3790
(979) 778-1082
www.asca.org

U.S. Border Collie Handler's Association
Francis Raley, Secretary
2915 Anderson Ln.
Crawford, TX 76638
(254) 486-2500
www.usbcha.com

Flyball
North American Flyball Association
1400 W. Devon Ave. #512
Chicago, IL 60660
(800) 318-6312
www.flyball.org

Freestyle
Musical Canine Sports International
Sharon Tutt
Treasurer/Membership
16665 Parkview Place
Surrey, BC V4N 1Y8
Canada
(604) 581-3641
www.dog-play.com/
musical.html

World Canine Freestyle Organization
P.O. Box 350122
Brooklyn, NY 11235-2525
(718) 332-8336
www.worldcanine
freestyle.org

Therapy Certification
Delta Society
875 124 Ave. NE, Suite 101
Bellevue, WA 98005-2521
(423) 226-7357
www.deltasociety.org

Therapy Dogs International
88 Bartley Rd.
Flanders, NJ 07836
(973) 252-9800
www.tdi-dog.org

Tracking
American Kennel Club
5580 Centerview Dr.
Suite 200
Raleigh, NC 27606
(919) 233-9780
www.akc.org

United Schutzhund Clubs of America
3810 Paule Ave.
St. Louis, MO 63125-1718
(314) 638-9686
www.germanshepherd.com

Other
American Mixed Breed Obedience Registry
179 Niblick Rd. #113
Paso Robles, CA 93446
(805) 226-9275
www.amborusa.org

Canadian Kennel Club
89 Skyway Ave., Unit 100
Etobicoke, ON M9W 6R4
Canada
(800) 250-8040
www.ckc.ca

Electric Fences/
Behavior Management Systems

■ **Invisible Fence** was the first underground electronic fence to appear on the market more than twenty-five years ago. It is marketed only through IF dealers, and each system is totally customized. For dealers or more information, see **www.invisiblefence.com** or call (800) 538-3647 (U.S.) or (800) 661-6286 (Canada).

■ **Innotek** offers a wide variety of features for sites up to three acres. The company also has pet barrier, no bark, and sporting dog training systems. See **www.innotek.net** or call (800) 826-5527.

■ **Radio Fence** offers a wireless and underground systems. See **www.radiofence.com** or call (800) 941-4200 or (941) 505-8220.

■ **Animal Behavior Systems** is the originator of citronella training systems in the United States. The products are available from owner Premier Pet Products as well as veterinarians, trainers, and shelters. ABS products all employ the same basic technology—the dog wears a nylon collar with a sensor unit attached, and a pressurized reservoir filled with citronella. When the sensor unit is triggered it releases a brisk citronella spray in front of the dog's nose. The spray is a natural, non-toxic liquid that distracts the dog from the inappropriate behavior and acts as a mild aversive. The dog hears, sees, feels and smells the spray and finds the experience distasteful, and soon learns which behaviors to stop to avoid triggering the spray. See **www.animalbehaviorsystems.com** or call (800) 640-8840.

Collars, Harnesses, & Leads

For a more in-depth discussion of collars, harnesses, and leads, see chapters 15 and 16. Prices and size, color, and style availability can vary among retailers.

■ **The Holt Control** harness is worth trying, especially for dogs who don't like head collars.

■ **The Pro-Stop!** harness is well-made, but more complicated to put on the dog than the Holt. It also accommodates larger sizes than the Holt.

- **The SENSE-ation** harness is relatively new and has received numerous positive reviews. It applies horse training concepts and comes with a training guide. The harness consists of a nylon loop just behind the dog's front legs and a connecting strap across the dog's chest. See **www.softouchconcepts.com**.

- **The Sof-Touch** leash, developed by trainer William E. Campbell, is a simple six-foot nylon leash with a short piece of elastic stitched and snapped in to create a shock absorber. The elastic piece tightens gradually muting the impact of the dog hitting the end of the leash. See **www.softouchconcepts.com**.

- **The Gentle Leader** head collar comes in a variety of colors and sizes and was developed by Dr. R.K. Anderson, an American College of Veterinary Behavior diplomate, and Ruth Foster.

- **The Snoot Loop** head collar was developed by Dr. Peter Borchelt, an applied animal behaviorist. It's the best bet going for brachycephalic dogs. The design works for a variety of head shapes (a strength compared with similar products), but it does take a bit of patience to adjust this head collar because of the need to knot the noseband. See **www.snootloop.com**.

- **The Halti** head collar was developed in England and is sturdier than the Snoot Loop.

- **The Lupine** safety collars, harnesses and leads come in a variety of sizes and colors. See **www.lupinepet.com** or call (800) 228-9653.

Media

Books

- *Clicker Training for Obedience Competition: Shaping Top Performance—Positively* by Morgan Spector (Sunshine Books, 1999; $29.95). This is a great choice for the serious obedience competitor who wants to maintain a positive relationship with his or her dog based on partnership and cooperation rather than punishment and intimidation, and still be in the running for those perfect 200 obedience scores.

- *Clicking With Your Dog* by Peggy Tillman (Sunshine Books, 2001; 24.95). The best book for novice owners, Tillman offers step-by-step instruction accompanied by pictures using clicker training to teach obedience, tricks, and manners.

■ *Culture Clash* by Jean Donaldson (James & Kenneth, 1997; $17.95).
Donaldson, a well-known trainer and speaker, offers insights into
the way your dog views the training process. Also from Donaldson: *Dogs Are From Neptune* (Lasar Multimedia Productions, 1998;
$16.95). This book consists of Donaldson's answers to questions
from owners with dog behavior problems, with heavy emphasis
on aggression.

■ *Getting Started: Clicker Training for Dogs,* 3rd edition, by Karen
Pryor (Sunshine Books, 2002; $14.95). The author is a leading pro-
ponent of clicker training; her Web site, **www.clickertraining.com**,
provides information about events, products and training.

■ *The Irrepressible Toy Dog* by Darlene Arden (Howell Books, 1998;
$17.95). This book is laden with information about the raising
and keeping of toy dogs. Arden incorporates some current thinking on positive reinforcement and clicker training, but is too
quick, in our opinion, to counsel the use of an aversive "No!" for
puppies.

■ *The Other End of the Leash* by Patricia McConnell (Ballantine,
2002; $25.95). McConnell offers an ethological perspective of dog
behavior. It's a must, in our opinion, for owners to understand why
dogs do what they do.

Videos
■ *Click & Go: Clicker Fun With Dr. Deborah Jones* (1999; $29.95).
Jones is a psychologist, member of the Association of
Pet Dog Trainers, and a trainer. She offers short verbal explana-
tions followed by hands-on demonstrations with happy dogs
who are eager to show off their abilities. Also: *Click & Fetch:
Clicker Fun With Dr. Deborah Jones* (1999; $29.95). See
www.caninetraining.com.

■ *Click and Treat Training Kit* (1996; $49.95). Trainer Gary Wilkes
offers a kit that includes an instruction book and two clickers. See
www.clickandtreat.com.

■ *Clicker Magic* (1997; $39.95). This Karen Pryor video is a delight-
ful collection of actual clicker training sessions, some with Pryor,
some with other trainers.

■ *Dancing With Your Dog: Getting Started* (1997; $29.95). Musical canine freestyle, or dancing with your dog,combines basic training exercises such as heel, sit and lie down. Sandra Davis also includes a series of flashier moves choreographed into a routine by the individual dog owner. Also from Davis: *Dancing With Your Dog: Getting the Rhythm* (1997; $29.95) and *Dancing With Your Dog: Getting Applause* (1998; $29.95). See **www.dancingdogs.net**.

■ *Dogs, Cats & Kids* (1996; $19.95). Pet behavior specialist and veterinarian Wayne Hunthausen teaches children and adults the correct way to approach and handle pets, how to read body language, when to leave an animal alone, and what to do about strays. It succeeds in instilling respect for animals without creating fear.

■ *Frisbee Dogs: Throwing Video* (1996; $24.95). Canine Frisbee champion Peter Bloeme teaches owners how to throw to throw the disc, demonstrates a variety of grips and throws, explains how to motivate an unenthusiastic Frisbee student (canine), and offers a "health and hazard advisory.

■ *"Paw-sitive" Dog Training* (1998; $29.95). Trainer and former Association of Pet Dog Trainers President Allan Bauman shows how to use lure and reward methods effectively to teach basic training exercises. See **www.dogwise.com**.

■ *Sirius Puppy Training* (updated 2004; $29.95). This tape with Dr. Ian Dunbar is a must-have for the family who has recently acquired a new puppy or is thinking about getting one. Dunbar was one of the pioneers of reward-based dog training in the United States, and is the founder of the Association of Pet Dog Trainers. The tape is full of entertaining demonstrations of real-life puppy training, handling, and gentling, and emphasizes the importance of family participation in the training process. Also with Dunbar: *Training Dogs With Dunbar* (2004; $24.95).

■ *Take a Bow ... WOW!* (1995; $24.95). Trainers Virginia Broitman and Sherri Lippman emphasize the importance of having fun with your dog when you train and demonstrate how to use positive reinforcement methods to teach behaviors such as take a bow, play dead, ring a bell, roll over, open and more. Also from Broitman: *Bow WOW, Take 2* (1997; $24.95).

■ *Training Dogs With John Fisher* (1995; $21.95). The late British consultant shares advice. Also from Fisher: *Training the Dog in the Human Pack* (1995; $21.95). See **www.dogwise.com**.

"Food" Toys

Throughout this book, we've frequently recommended that you place kibble or treats into toys as part of the training process. Some brands follow; you will find them and others at many pet care stores.

■ **Kong** toys, made from natural rubber, come in all sorts of shapes and sizes. They're great for challenging your dog to get out all the kibble, peanut butter, and other treats you stuff inside.

■ **Boomer balls** are based on the same premise as Kong toys. These rigid plastic have holes drilled into them so that you can push in treats and kibble and keep your dog challenged, occupied, and rewarded.

■ **Busy Buddy** chew toys, a new line from Premier Pet Products (home of the Gentle Leader head collar) includes Twist 'n Treat, Groove Thing, Chuckle, Waggle and Biscuit Bouncer footballs. Premier says each toy was designed with a different chewing experience in mind and aims to turn potentially destructive chewing into positive playtime. See **www.busybuddytoys.com**.

Additional Resources

■ **Animal Behavior Associates**, Drs. Suzanne Hetts' and Dan Estep's consultancy, offers a free monthly e-newsletter as well as numerous online resources for solving common pet behavior problems. ■

Index